じっぴコンパクト文庫

英語対訳で読む科学の疑問

松森靖夫

監修

Steve Mills

英文監訳

実業之日本社

装幀●杉本欣右
イラスト●笹森　識
日本文執筆●中村英良＋森井美紀
DTP・編集●スタジオスパーク
協力●オフィスON

はじめに /PREFACE

　私たちの身の周りには、さまざまな『疑問』が満ちあふれています。その中には、知っているようで本当は知らないこと、答えられそうで実はなかなかうまく答えられないものがあります。

　たとえば、「宇宙の果ては、どうなっているの?」、「空はなぜ、青いの?」、「動物にはなぜ、雄と雌がいるの?」、「人間はどうして、必ず死ぬの?」、「携帯電話はなぜ、つながるの?」……などなど。

　本書では、そうした素朴だけれど、答えに窮するようないろいろな疑問について、科学の眼を通して解明しています。しかも、それを平易な日本語と中学レベルのやさしい英語でダブル解説するという、初めての試みの本です。

　宇宙や地球に関すること、私たち人間を含めた生き物に対すること、また、私たちの体についてのこと、そのほか、私たちの生活全般にかかわることなど、79項目を取り上げました。

　構成については、「問」に対する「答」というスタイルにし、答えに関して諸説あるものについては、代表的なもの、最新の学説を優先しました。ですから、本書で解説した答えが唯一無二のものではなく、ほかの回答や学説がある場合もあることをお断りしておきます。

　また、英文と日本文の両方に番号を振ってあるので、読者のみなさんが英文を読んでいてわからないところが出てきたときには、対応する日本文がすぐに見つけられるようになっています。

　英語学習には、テーマや内容の面白さがないと、なかなか長続きしないものです。その意味からも、興味が尽きない本書の「科学の疑問」を読みながら、知らず知らずのうちに英語に強くなっていただければ、これに過ぎる喜びはありません。

　なお、本書作成にあたっては、山梨大学の理科のプロフェッショナルである松森靖夫先生、およびスティーブ・ミルズ氏の監修を仰ぎました。この場を借りて、厚くお礼申し上げます。

PREFACE / はじめに

There are various questions which we can not understand around us. Some of them are the questions which we think we understand but actually we do not understand and which we think we can answer but actually we can not answer well.

Some examples of them are "What is there at the end of the universe?", "Why does the sky look blue?", "Why do animals have two sexes, male and female?", "Why must all human beings die?", "How are cell-phones connected?", and so on.

Such questions, which are simple but we can not answer well, are scientifically clarified in this book. Furthermore, this is the first book to answer the questions both in simple Japanese and in simple English, which even junior high school students may understand.

79 topics about universe, the earth, creatures including human beings, our body, and many things in our daily life are picked up.

This book adopts the questions and answers style. When a question has various believable answers, the typical and latest theory is introduced. Therefore note that the answer introduced in this book is not the only one and some questions have many other answers and theories.

Every Japanese and English sentence is numbered in this book. Therefore when you have difficulty in reading the English sentences, you can find their Japanese translation in no time.

You may give up studying English easily if the textbook does not have interesting subjects and contents. From this point of view, it would be more than happy if you can brush up your English unconsciously by reading the very interesting science questions and answers in this book.

In closing, in the course of making this book, Professor Matsumori Yasuo of University of Yamanashi, the specialist in science supervised the Japanese part and Mr. Steve Mills supervised the English part of this book. I would like to express special thanks to them all.

CONTENTS / 目次

Chapter 1

Questions about the universe/ 宇宙の疑問

1 When and how the universe was born?
   宇宙はいつ、どのようにしてできたの? *12*

2 What is there at the end of the universe?
   宇宙の果てはどうなっているの? *14*

3 Is there any planet human beings can live on in space?
   宇宙に人間が住める星はあるの? *16*

4 Why is the sun burning all the time?
   太陽はどうして、ずっと燃えているの? *18*

5 Why is the earth moving around the sun?
   地球は太陽の周りを、どうして回っているの? *20*

6 Why is the earth rotating?
   地球はなぜ、自転しているの? *24*

7 Why are the earth, the sun, and the moon spheres?
   なぜ、地球も太陽も月も丸いの? *26*

8 Why don't people and things on the other side of the earth
   fall off even though they are upside-down?|
   なぜ、地球の反対側の人や物は上下逆さなのに落ちないの? *28*

9 Why does the moon change its shape?
   なぜ、月の形は変化するの? *30*

10 Why does the moon keep up with us when we are walking?
   歩いていると、なぜ月はついてくるの? *32*

11 Why do shooting stars fall?
   流れ星はどうして流れるの? *36*

12 Why do stars shine?
   なぜ、星は光るの? *38*

Chapter 2

Questions about the earth/ 地球の疑問

13 Why does the sky look blue?
   空はどうして青いの? *42*

14	Why are sunsets red? 夕焼けはなぜ、赤いの？	*44*
15	Why is seawater salty? 海水はなぜ、塩辛いの？	*46*
16	Why is a mountain top colder though it is nearer to the sun? 山の上は太陽に近いのに、どうして寒いの？	*48*
17	How are auroras formed? オーロラはどうやってできるの？	*50*
18	Does air have weight? 空気に重さはあるの？	*52*
19	How do earthquakes happen? 地震はどうして起きるの？	*56*
20	How were the deserts formed? 砂漠はどうやってできたの？	*58*
21	Which is colder, the North Pole or the South Pole? 北極と南極では、どちらが寒いの？	*60*
22	Why doesn't lake water soak into the bottom? 湖の水はどうして、底にしみ込まないの？	*62*
23	Why are snow crystals hexagonal? 雪の結晶はなぜ、六角形なの？	*64*
24	Why does it snow though the temperature is not below 0 degrees C? 気温が零度以下ではなくても、なぜ雪が降るの？	*68*

Chapter 3

Questions about creatures / 生き物の疑問

25	Why did the dinosaurs die out? 恐竜はなぜ、絶滅したの？	*72*
26	Why do animals have two sexes, male and female? 動物はなぜ、雄と雌に分かれているの？	*74*
27	Why can sparrows perch on electric wires? スズメはなぜ、電線にとまっても平気なの？	*76*

CONTENTS / 目次

28　Why do migratory birds fly in a V-formation?
渡り鳥はどうして、Vの字になって飛ぶの？　*78*

29　Fish don't close their eyes but don't they sleep?
魚は眼を閉じないけれど、寝ないの？　*82*

30　Why can salmon live both in the sea and the rivers?
サケはどうして、海と川の両方で生きていけるの？　*84*

31　Don't lions become sick though they eat only meat, not vegetables?
ライオンは肉ばかり食べて野菜を食べなくても、病気にならないの？　*86*

32　Why do sunflowers always face to the sun?
ヒマワリの花はどうして、太陽のほうをむいているの？　*88*

33　Why don't penguins live in the North Pole?
ペンギンはどうして、北極にはいないの？　*92*

34　Why do ants walk in line?
アリはどうして、行列をつくって歩くの？　*94*

35　Why aren't deep-sea fish crushed under water pressure?
深海魚はなぜ、水圧に押しつぶされないの？　*96*

36　Why do leaves turn red in autumn?
秋になると、なぜ葉っぱが赤くなるの？　*98*

Chapter 4

Questions about human body/ 人間の体の疑問

37　Did human beings evolve from apes?
ヒトはサルから進化したの？　*104*

38　Why must all human beings die?
人間はなぜ、必ず死ぬの？　*106*

39　Why isn't the human body covered with hair like dogs or cats?
ヒトはどうして、イヌやネコのように全身が毛で覆われていないの？　*108*

40　Why do you shed tears when you are sad?
なぜ、悲しいと涙が出るの？　*110*

41　Why can you drink many glasses of beer in a short time?
どうして、ビールは何杯も飲めるの？　*112*

42	Why does alcohol make people drunk? 酒を飲むと、どうして酔っぱらうの?	114
43	Why are feces brown? ウンチはどうして、茶色なの?	118
44	Why do we dream? 人はなぜ、夢を見るの?	120
45	Why do we have fever, cough, and a sore throat when we catch cold? 風邪をひくと、なぜ熱やせきが出たり、のどが痛くなったりするの?	122
46	Why does a headache go away with medicine taken through the mouth? 口から飲んだ薬で、なぜ頭痛が治るの?	124
47	Why doesn't the stomach wall dissolve in stomach acid? 胃の壁はなぜ、胃酸で溶けないの?	126
48	Why does the head hurt after eating shaved ice? かき氷を食べると、なぜ頭痛がするの?	128
49	Why do you have white hair? なぜ、白髪になるの?	132
50	Where do baby's feces go in the mother's body? お腹の中の赤ちゃんのウンチは、どうなっているの?	134
51	Why don't human beings breathe in water? 人はどうして、水の中で息ができないの?	136
52	How do you find a criminal by a fingerprint? 指紋でなぜ、犯人が見つかるの?	138
53	Why don't we see things double though we have two eyes? 眼は二つあるのに、なぜものが一つに見えるの?	140
54	Why can you see clearly with glasses? メガネをかけると、なぜよく見えるようになるの?	142
55	How do you check the blood types, A, B, O, and AB? どうやって、A、B、O、ABの血液型を調べるの?	146

CONTENTS / 目次

Chapter 5

Questions about the things around us/ 身の周りの疑問

56 Why can microwave ovens heat up food?
電子レンジでどうして、料理が温まるの？
150

57 Why do eggs get hard when they are boiled?
卵はどうして、ゆでると固くなるの？
152

58 Why does plastic cling film stick to something?
ラップはなぜ、ぴったりくっつくの？
154

59 Why do tears come in your eyes when you slice an onion?
タマネギを刻むと、どうして涙が出るの？
156

60 Why does food go bad?
食べ物はなぜ、腐るの？
158

61 Why is a drainpipe s-shaped?
排水管の形はなぜ、S字型なの？
160

62 What is the real color of shrimps?
エビの色は、本当は何色なの？
164

63 What is the difference between fish with white meat and fish with red meat?
白身の魚と赤身の魚は、どう違うの？
166

64 Why do things burn when they are set on fire?
火をつけると、なぜ物が燃えるの？
168

65 Why don't pickled plums go bad though they are not dry?
梅干しは乾燥しているわけでもないのに、なぜ腐らないの？
170

66 Why water changes to ice when it is cooled?
水を冷やすと、なぜ氷になるの？
172

67 Why does it get cold in the refrigerator?
冷蔵庫はどうして、冷えるの？
174

68 How can you see yourself in a mirror?
なぜ、鏡に姿が映るの？
178

69 How does detergent remove dirt?
洗剤はどうやって、汚れを落とすの？
180

70 Why can erasers erase letters?
どうして、消しゴムで字が消せるの？
182

CONTENTS / 目次

71 Why can an iron smooth wrinkles?
アイロンをかけると、なぜシワが伸びるの？ *184*

72 Why does a magnet attract iron?
なぜ、鉄と磁石はくっつくの？ *188*

73 Why does it become white when light's three primary colors are mixed?
光の三原色を合わせると、なぜ白くなるの？ *190*

74 Why don't you get burned in a sauna bath?
なぜ、サウナでヤケドしないの？ *192*

75 Why do clock hands move to the right?
時計の針はどうして、右回りなの？ *194*

76 Why does a playback of your recorded voice sound strange?
どうして、録音した自分の声は変なの？ *198*

77 How are cell-phones connected?
携帯電話はどうして、つながるの？ *200*

78 How can airplanes fly?
飛行機はなぜ、飛ぶことができるの？ *202*

79 Is it possible to make a time machine?
タイムマシンはつくれるの？ *206*

Chapter 1

Questions about the universe

第 1 章
宇宙の疑問

Qustions and answers about science

When and how the universe was born?

①Various hypotheses have been proposed to explain how the universe was born. ②The most popular among them is the Big Bang theory. ③According to this theory, the universe was originally an extremely small dot, which was red hot and high dense. ④This theory says that the dot began to get bigger and bigger very rapidly in time and space as if it had blown up, and then the universe was born.

⑤In many different ways, scientists are studying about when the universe was born. ⑥An electromagnetic wave named CMB (cosmic microwave background radiation) played an important part in their studies. ⑦CMB is a very old electromagnetic wave like a fossil sent out soon after the universe was born and it reaches the earth from all around the space even today.

⑧ NASA (National Aeronautics and Space Administration)

12

第1章　宇宙の疑問

launched a microwave observatory satellite to
〜を打ち上げた　マイクロ波を観測する衛星　　　　〜を観測するために
monitor CMB. ⑨The results of analysis show that the
　　　　　　　　　　〜の分析結果
universe wasborn about 13.7 billion years ago. (see p.22)
　　　　　　　　　　　137億年前

問1　　**宇宙はいつ、どのようにしてできたの？**

答　①宇宙の成立については、さまざまな仮説が、立てられてきました。②その中で現在一番広く受け入れられているのが「ビッグバン理論」です。

③このビッグバン理論では、宇宙の始まりはとてつもなく高温、高密度で限りなく小さい、点のようなかたまりです。④これがあたかも爆発したかのように急激に時間と空間の拡張を始め、宇宙が生まれたとされています。

⑤宇宙誕生の時期についてもさまざまな研究がなされています。⑥この研究に貢献したのは CMB（宇宙マイクロ波背景放射）という電磁波でした。⑦CMB は宇宙が誕生して間もない頃に出された化石のような電磁波であり、現在でも宇宙のあらゆる方向から地球に届いています。

⑧NASA（米航空宇宙局）は CMB を観測するために、マイクロ波観測衛星を打ち上げました。⑨その結果の解析から、宇宙は約 137 億年前に生まれたとされています。

13

Q2 What is there at the end of the universe?

①First of all, how far into space can we see? ②It is said that the universe was born around 13.7 billion years ago. ③Since the distance that light travels in a year is called a light year, the light the earth catches now was given off 13.7 billion years ago by stars 13.7 billion light years away. ④Therefore we should be able to see 13.7 billion light years away.

⑤In 1929, an American astronomer, Edwin Hubble, found that the universe is continuing to expand. ⑥He said that all the stars in the universe are moving away from the earth, and that the further a star is from the earth, the faster it moves.

⑦To sum up, if we think of the end of the universe as the furthest point we can see, it is 13.7 billion light years away now and it is still extending. ⑧When we think of the end of the universe as the limit of space, not as the furthest point

14

第1章　宇宙の疑問

we can see, we can not even find yet whether there is an
　　　　　　　　　　　　　　　　　　　　〜であるかどうか
end to it or not.

問2　　　　宇宙の果てはどうなっているの？

答 ①まず、宇宙はどこまで見えるかを考えてみましょう。②宇宙が誕生したのは約137億年前といわれています。③光が1年間に進む距離を1光年といいますので、137億光年離れた星が137億年前に発した光が、今やっと地球に届いていることになります。④現在の地球からどこまで見渡せるかを考えると、137億光年の彼方まで、ということになります。
⑤1929年には、アメリカのエドウィン・ハッブルという学者が、宇宙は膨張し続けていることを発見しました。⑥銀河のすべての星が地球から遠ざかるように動き、その速度は地球からその星までの距離に比例して速くなるというのです。
⑦つまり、宇宙の果てが「見える限界」と考えると、現在は137億光年彼方であり、刻々と広がり続けていることになります。⑧見える限界ではなく、空間としての限界ということになると、今のところ宇宙の果てが存在しているかどうかさえ、わかっていません。

Q3 Is there any planet human beings can live on in space?

①A planet on which human beings can live must
　　　　人類が住むことのできる惑星
meet certain conditions, for example it must have
　～にかなう　　条件
water, it must have a temperature similar to that of the earth, it
　　　　　　　　　　　　　　地球と似た気温
must be made up of rock and metal, and so on. ②In the solar
　　～からできている　　　　　　　　　　　　　　　太陽系で
system Mars meets some of these conditions. ③However, the
　　　火星
average temperature on Mars is low, around minus 60 degrees
平均気温　　　　　　　　　　　　　　　摂氏マイナス60度
Celsius, and about more than 90 percent of its atmosphere
　　　　　　　　　　　　　　　　　　　　　　　　大気
consists of carbon dioxide. ④Therefore human beings can not
～からなる　二酸化炭素
live on Mars.

⑤Then, how about outside this solar system? ⑥The earth
　　　　　　　　　～の外側
is a planet moving around the sun, a fixed star. ⑦Apart
　　　　　　　　　　　　　　　　　　恒星　　　　　～以外にも
from the sun, there are countless fixed stars which give off
　　　　　　　　　　　無数の　　　　　　　　　　～を放つ
light on their own out there in the universe. ⑧There
　　　　　　　　　　　　　宇宙全体の中に
could be some planets around these fixed stars which have

a similer environment to that of the earth.
地球と似た環境
⑨For example, there is a planet named Gliese 581 d, which
　　　　　　　　　　　　　　　　　　　　グリーゼ581d

16

moves around a fixed star, Gliese 581, 20.4 light-years away
(～から20.4光年離れた)
from the solar system. ⑩Based on the nature of Gliese 581,
(性質)
the Sun-like star, and the distance between Gliese 581 and
(距離)
Gliese 581d, it appears that there may be some water on
(～のようだ)
Gliese 581d which would be essential for some organisms
(～が～するのに欠くことのできない) (生物)
to live there.

問3　宇宙に人間が住める星はあるの？

答 ①人間が住める星には、水がある、気温が地球に近い、岩石や金属などでできているなど、いくつかの条件があります。②太陽系でこの条件に近い星は火星です。③しかし、平均気温がマイナス60度前後と低く、大気の90パーセント以上は二酸化炭素です。④これでは、人間が住めそうにもありません。⑤では、太陽系以外ではどうでしょうか？　⑥地球は、恒星である太陽の周りを回っている惑星です。⑦広い宇宙には、太陽のほかにも、自ら光を放つ星である恒星が無数に存在します。⑧その周りには、地球と同じような環境の惑星が存在する可能性は十分にあります。

⑨たとえば、太陽系から20.4光年離れたグリーゼ581という名前の恒星の周りを回る惑星、グリーゼ581dです。⑩太陽にあたるグリーゼ581の性質や、そこからの距離で、グリーゼ581dには生命の生存に欠かせない水があると考えられています。

Why is the sun burning all the time?

①Like the other fixed stars, the sun also gives off large amounts of energy and light by a nuclear fusion reaction of hydrogen to form helium. ②The sun is about 109 times the diameter of the earth and it is thought that about 90 percent of the mass of the sun is hydrogen. ③Scientists say that as much as about 700 million tons of hydrogen is used for the nuclear fusion reaction per second at the center of the sun.

④However, the sun will not go on shining forever like today. ⑤When there is little hydrogen left and helium comes to the center of the sun, the nuclear fusion reaction of hydrogen outside speeds up and expands outward. ⑥It is called a red giant. ⑦After that, those gases flow out and it becomes a white dwarf, which has no nuclear fusion reactions, and it then takes billions of years to become cold. ⑧The sun, which is thought will exist for around 10 billion

第1章　宇宙の疑問

years, is now about 4.7 billion years old. ⑨Therefore the
4.7億歳

sun will shine as it does today for billions of years more.
今日のように　　　　　　あと数十億年間

(see p.23)

問4　太陽はどうして、ずっと燃えているの？

答　①太陽もほかの恒星と同じように、水素がヘリウムに変化する核融合反応によって大量のエネルギーを発生し、光を放っています。②直径が地球の約109倍もある巨大な太陽ですが、その質量の90パーセント程度が水素だと考えられています。③中心では、毎秒約7億トンもの水素が核融合反応によって消費されているといわれています。
④しかし、太陽はずっと今のように輝き続けるわけではありません。⑤水素が残り少なくなると、ヘリウムが中心に集まり、その外側にある水素の核融合が加速して外側に広がっていきます。⑥これが赤色巨星です。⑦その後、ガスが流出して核融合反応が起こらない白色矮星となり、数十億年かけて冷えていきます。
⑧寿命100億年前後と考えられている太陽は、現在約47億歳です。⑨そのため、あと数十億年は、今の状態で輝き続けることでしょう。

19

Why is the earth moving around the sun?

①Everything in this universe has the power to
引きつける力
pull all other things, and the things which has a
ほかのあらゆるもの   より質量が大きいものほど
larger mass have stronger power. ②This is called the

universal gravitation.
万有引力
③Put a strong magnet on the ground and roll an iron ball
強力な磁石   ～を転がす 鉄の玉
near the magnet. ④The iron ball will not go straight

because the strong magnet will pull it. ⑤The iron ball will

change direction a little or go straight to the magnet
少し方向を変える   まっすぐ～へ向かう
depending on the strength of the magnet and the distance
～しだいで   ～の強さ   ～の間の距離
between these two things.

⑥The iron ball may move around the magnet under certain
        ～かもしれない ～の周りを回る   ある特定の条件のもとでは
conditions, such as the weight of the iron ball, its speed and
            たとえば ～の重量   その速度
the strength of the magnet. ⑦Planets such as the earth and
                            惑星
others in the solar system can be thought of in this way.
              太陽系   このように
⑧The earth moves around the sun because of the
                                    ～のために
gravitational pull of the sun and the inertia which the earth
～の引力   慣性

20

第1章　宇宙の疑問

itself has: a property that keeps itself moving.
　　　　　　自らを動かし続ける特性

問5　地球は太陽の周りを、どうして回っているの？

答　①この宇宙では、どんなものにも、ほかのものを引きつける力があり、その力は質量が大きくなるほど、大きなものになります。②これが万有引力です。
③強力な磁石を置き、その近くで鉄の玉を転がすとします。④鉄の玉は磁石の方向に引っ張られ、まっすぐに転がらないでしょう。⑤磁石の強さや鉄の玉と磁石の距離によって、方向を変えて転がっていってしまったり、そのまま磁石に引き寄せられたりします。
⑥鉄の玉の重量と、磁石の強さ、転がした速度によって、磁石の周りを回る動きを見せる場合もあります。⑦これが地球などの惑星と考えていいでしょう。
⑧地球は、地球自体が持つ慣性、つまり動き続けようとする性質と、太陽の引力によって公転しているのです。

宇宙は137億年前、爆発（ビッグバン）によって生まれた

The universe was born 13.7 billion years ago by an explosion called the Big Bang.

宇宙の初期のころ
The early stages of the universe

宇宙の初期は高温、高密度な一点だったと考えられている。
The universe in the early stage is thought to have been a red-hot and high-density dot.

ビッグバン
The Big Bang

小さな点だった初期宇宙が、あたかも爆発のように大きく膨張し始めた。
The early universe as a dot began to extend as if it had blown up.

宇宙の果ては137億光年の彼方

The end of the universe is 13.7 billion light years away.

137億年前（宇宙の誕生時）に、137億光年の彼方で発生した光などの電磁波が、現在の地球に届いている。
Electromagnetic waves such as light given off 13.7 billion years ago, at birth of the universe, 13.7 billion light years away reach the earth now.

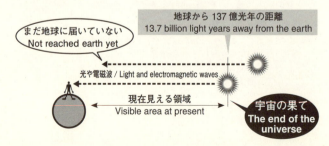

太陽はやがて燃え尽きる
The sun will burn out some day

現在の太陽
Today's sun

赤色巨星
Red giant

水素が残り少なくなると、外側にある水素の核融合が加速して外側に広がる
When there is little hydrogen left, the nuclear fusion reaction of hydrogen outside speeds up and expands outward.

ガスを放出する
Giving off gases

中心は自らの重力で収縮し、外側を覆うガスは離れていく
The center of it contracts by its own gravity and the gases covering it flow out.

白色矮星
White dwarf

外側のガスがなくなり、地球ほどの大きさになった中心部が白色矮星となる
The gases which covered it flow out and the center of it becomes as small as the earth and a white dwarf.

Q6 Why is the earth rotating?

①Gases, dust and small planets were moving around like "an eddying current" when the sun was born. ②Since the gases, the dust and the small planets grew bigger as they continued to run into one after another, the planets of the solar system, including the earth, were born.

③When two balls run into each other, they sometimes rotate. ④This happens when the two balls do not collide, head-on, but just brush each other. ⑤The earth came to rotate one time in about 23 hours 56 minutes 4.06 seconds as it does today after continuing to run into other planets and so on again and again.

⑥A rotating ball will stop after a while because of the friction between the ball and the ground. ⑦However, the earth floating in the universe, which is almost a vacuum, has no friction to stop it from rotating. ⑧Therefore the earth keeps rotating as long as there is no collision with

第1章　宇宙の疑問

great force, such as a planet. ⑨There are in fact some forces
大きな力　　　　　　　　　　　　　　実際には

which impede the rotation of the earth such as the friction
　　　　妨げる

between the tides and the sea bottom among other things.
潮の干満と海底との間の

⑩As a result, the rotation of the earth slows down about
　そのため

one over one hundred thousand seconds every year.
10万分の1秒

問6　地球はなぜ、自転しているの？

答 ①太陽が誕生したとき、ガスや塵、小さな惑星が渦を巻いて回っていました。②それらが衝突を繰り返しながら大きくなり、地球をはじめとする太陽系の惑星が生まれました。③二つのボールがぶつかると、回転することがあります。④真正面からぶつからず、中心からはずれてかすったような場合です。⑤地球も、惑星などとの衝突を繰り返すうちに、現在のように約23時間56分4.06秒周期で自転するようになりました。⑥ボールは回転しても、地面に接している面で抵抗があるため、やがて止まってしまいます。⑦ところが、真空にほぼ近い宇宙に浮かぶ地球に対しては、回転を妨げる抵抗がありません。⑧そのため、惑星との衝突といった大きな力が加わらない限り、回転し続けます。⑨ただし、地球にも、潮の干満と海底との摩擦など、自転を妨げる力が働いています。⑩そのため、1年間に約10万分の1秒ずつ自転速度が遅くなっています。

25

Q7 Why are the earth, the sun, and the moon spheres?

①Almost all the stars, including the earth, the sun, and the moon, are spherical in shape. ②This is the result of gravity.
③Various substances floating in the universe are put together by gravity and a star is born. ④In any case, gravity pulls things toward its center. ⑤If a star had the shape of a cube, its vertexes would have weaker gravity as they are far from its center and the part around its center would have stronger gravity as it is near its center. ⑥In a sphere, the distance between its center and any points on its surface is the same. ⑦Therefore any points on its surface have the same gravity. ⑧Some newborn stars are not spherical in shape, but even such stars gradually become spheres because of gravity in the course of time. ⑨Some minor planets with low mass do not become perfect balls because of their weak gravity. ⑩The minor planet named Toutatis,

26

第1章　宇宙の疑問

which came dangerously near to the earth in November
　　　　　　危険なくらい近くに
2008, is only 4.9 km long even at its longest point. ⑪It was
　　　　　　　　　　　　　最も長い部分でも
oval in shape, resembling the shape of two combined stars,
楕円形の　　　　～に似ている　　　　　　　　　合体した2つの星
by observed through a telescope. (see p.34)
　　　　　　　　望遠鏡

問7　なぜ、地球も太陽も月も丸いの？

答 ①地球、太陽、月に限らず、ほとんどの星は球の形をしています。②これは、重力によるものです。

③重力によって宇宙をさまようさまざまな物質が集まり、星が生まれます。④重力は、常に中心にむかって働きます。⑤仮に星が立方体だとすると、中心から遠い角の部分は重力が弱くなり、中心に近い部分の重力が大きくなります。⑥球では、中心から表面のあらゆる地点までの距離が同じです。⑦そのため、表面のどの地点にも同じように重力が働きます。⑧生まれたばかりの星は球体でないこともありますが、時間がたつにつれ、重力によって球体になっていくのです。

⑨質量が小さい小惑星などの中には、重力が小さいために球体になりきれないものもあります。⑩2008年11月に地球に異常接近した小惑星トータティスは、一番長い部分でも４.９キロメートルしかありません。⑪望遠鏡がとらえたその姿は、楕円形に近い、二つの星が合体したようなものでした。

Q8. Why don't people and things on the other side of the earth fall off even though they are upside-down?

①The word "fall" expresses a movement from top to bottom. ②The South Pole of the earth is at the bottom of a model world globe, under which there is a pedestal. ③Even if you try to put a small doll on the South Pole of a model world globe, it will fall to the pedestal.

④However, this is the case of a model world globe, not the case of the real globe. ⑤This is why there is no concept of top and bottom in space.

⑥Now, let us think about what the word "bottom" means. ⑦You will soon find that we use "bottom" to express "the direction toward the ground". ⑧To be exact, the direction of gravity to pull things is the "bottom". ⑨Anywhere on the earth, gravity pulls things toward the center of the earth.

⑩"Falling" means a movement of things toward the center

第1章　宇宙の疑問

of the earth by the pull of gravity. ⑪In other words,
　　　　　　　　　　　　　　　　　　　言い換えると
everything falls toward the center of the earth even at the

South Pole though it is at the bottom of the world globe.

問8　なぜ、地球の反対側の人や物は上下逆さ
　　　　なのに落ちないの？

答　①私たちにとって、「落ちる」というのは、上から下に落ちることを意味します。②地球儀を見ると、南極は一番下のほうにあり、その下には地球儀を置いてある台座があります。③地球儀の南極に小さな人形を置こうとしても、下の台座のほうに落ちてしまうでしょう。

④しかし、これは机に置かれた地球儀であって、本物の地球となると話が違ってきます。⑤宇宙には、上も下もないからです。

⑥ここで、「下」とは何なのか考えてみましょう。⑦「下」というのは「地面がある方向」であることに気づくでしょう。⑧ちょっと難しい言い方をすれば、重力が働く方向が「下」です。⑨地球上のどこでも、重力は地球の中心付近にむかって働いています。

⑩「落ちる」とは、重力に引っぱられ地球の中心の方向にむかって移動することです。⑪つまり、地球儀の下にある南極であっても、ものは地球の中心にむかって落ちるのです。

Q9 Why does the moon change its shape?

①The moon is the nearest star to the earth of all
最も〜の近くにある星
the stars in solar system and it is the only satellite
〜の唯一の衛星
of the earth, which goes around it. ②The moon itself does
not give off light, but just seems to shine. ③The surface of
〜を放つ　　　　　輝いているように見えるだけ　〜の表面
the moon is covered with rocks which reflect sunlight in
〜で覆われている　　　　　　反射する　太陽の光
different directions and some of the light reaches the earth.
さまざまな方向に
④That is why the moon is not as bright as the sun.
そういうわけで　　　　　　〜ほど—ない
⑤Sunlight is parallel and strong. ⑥Therefore only half of
平行な
the surface of the moon reflects sunlight.

⑦It takes about four weeks for the moon to go around the
〜が—するのに—かかる
earth one time. ⑧While it goes around, the positions of the
〜の位置
sun, the earth, and the moon change. ⑨According to the
〜に従って
positions, the moon seen from the earth changes its shape
地球から見られた〜　　その形を変える
from new moon to half moon, and to full moon.
新月　　　　半月　　　　　　満月
⑩On the day when the moon and the sun are in the same
〜から見て同じ方向に
direction seen from the earth, the part of the moon lit by
〜の部分　　　太陽に照らされた〜
the sun can not be seen from the earth. ⑪In this case, only
〜から見られることができない　　　　このような場合において

30

第1章　宇宙の疑問

the outline of the moon or a very young moon can be seen.
~の輪郭だけ　　　　　　　　とても細い月

⑫This is called a new moon.

⑬The moon moves about 180 degrees in two weeks and, in
180度　　　　　2週間で

this case, only the part of the moon lit by the sun can be

seen from the earth. ⑭This is called a full moon. (see p.35)

問9　　　　　**なぜ、月の形は変化するの？**

答 ①月は太陽系の中でもっとも地球に近く、地球の周りを回っている唯一の衛星です。②月は自らが光っているのではなく、光っているように見えるだけです。③でこぼこした岩石で覆われた表面が太陽の光を乱反射し、その一部が地球に届くのです。④月が太陽ほど明るくないのは、このためです。

⑤太陽光は、平行で強い光です。⑥そのため、太陽の光を受けて光って見えるのは、月の半分だけです。

⑦月は地球の周りを約4週間かけて1回りします。⑧その間に、太陽、地球、月の位置関係は変わります。⑨この位置関係の変化により、地球から見た月は新月、半月、満月と形を変えるのです。

⑩地球から見て月と太陽が同じ方向にある日は、太陽光が当たっている部分が見えません。⑪地球からは月の輪郭、あるいはごく細い月がわずかに見えるだけです。⑫これが「新月」です。

⑬2週間ほどたつと月は約180度移動し、地球からは月の太陽が当たっている部分しか見えなくなります。⑬これが満月です。

Q10 Why does the moon keep up with us when we are walking?

①Suppose that you are walking along the street at night, and that, by the roadside, there is a telephone pole 10 meters ahead and an iron tower one kilometer ahead. ②When you walk 10 meters, you are just beside the telephone pole. ③At that time, the iron tower is 990 meters ahead of you and it looks almost like what you saw 10 meters behind. ④When you are moving, you feel that distant things do not change their position as much as nearby things.

⑤It is as far as 380 thousand kilometers from the earth to the moon. ⑥Even if you move a few kilometers, you do not feel that the position of the moon you see changes at all.

⑦In daily life, you do not feel that the position of a distant thing changes (a) when both you and the thing are moving at the same speed or (b) when both you and the thing are standing still. ⑧Since you supposed that you were walking

32

第1章　宇宙の疑問

along the street at night, it is clear that (b) is not the case
〜なのは明らかだ　　〜がここでの状況ではない
here. ⑨Therefore you get it wrong and think that the moon
　　　　　　　　　　　間違える
keeps up with you.
〜についてくる

問10　歩いていると、なぜ月はついてくるの？

答 ①たとえば、夜道を歩いていて 10 メートル前方の道路わきに電柱があり、1 キロ前方に鉄塔があったとします。②10 メートル進むと、あなたは電柱の真横にたどり着きます。③一方鉄塔は、990 メートル前方にあり、10 メートル前から見たのとほとんど変わっていないでしょう。④動いているあなたから見ると、遠くのものは近くのものに比べて位置変化が少なく感じられるのです。

⑤地球から月までの距離は 380,000 キロメートルもあります。⑥2 キロや 3 キロ移動したところで、あなたから見た月の位置はまったく変わりません。

⑦日常生活で、あなたと離れたものとの位置関係が変わらないのは、（a）両方とも同じ速度で移動しているか、（b）両方とも静止しているかのどちらかです。⑧あなたは夜道を歩いているので、（b）ではないことは明らかです。⑨そのため、月が同じように動いていると錯覚してしまうのです。

33

大きな天体が球形なのは、表面の重力が均等に働くから
Big stars are spherical in shape because any points on their surface have the same gravity.

球
Sphere

立方体
Cube

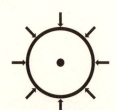

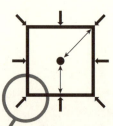

表面のどの場所でも、重力は均等に働く。
Any points on their surface have the same gravity.

中心に近いほど、大きな重力が働く。
The nearer the point comes to its center, the stronger gravity becomes.

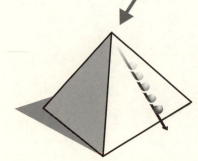

ものは重力が小さいところから大きいところへ移動しようとする。
Everything is always likely to move toward the point having strong gravity from the point having weak gravity.

その結果、全体に重力が均等な球形になる。
Therefore it became a sphere, which has the same gravity at any points on its surface.

34

月で光が当たっている部分は、地球との位置関係によって見え方が変わる

The part of the moon lit by the sun changes its shape according to the positions of the moon and the earth when we see from the earth.

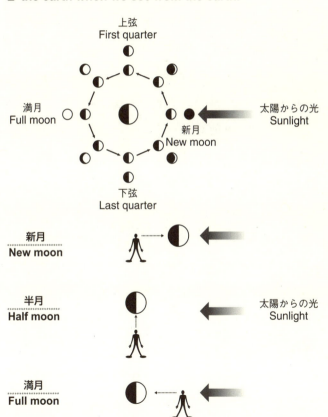

Q11 Why do shooting stars fall?

①Shooting stars are called "stars", but in fact they are not stars. ②They are small dust particles floating along the earth's orbital path. ③It is said that the smallest dust particle is about 0.1 millimeters across and even the biggest dust particle is only several centimeters across. ④These dust particles burn up and give off bright light after they enter the earth's atmosphere.

⑤Most of these dust particles, which could become shooting stars, were left by comets. ⑥A comet is like a mass of ice which has a lot of dust inside it. ⑦When comets are far from the sun, they are frozen hard. ⑧However, when they come nearer to the sun, they melt little by little and leave various substances behind. ⑨The vapor-trail-like substances left after a comet passes by are called "dust trails".

⑩Fine dust particles shower onto the earth when it goes through the "dust trail" left along its orbital path. ⑪As a

第1章　宇宙の疑問

result, a lot of shooting stars are seen from the earth.
その結果

問11　流れ星はどうして流れるの？

答　①流れ星は、流星と呼ばれますが星ではありません。②地球の公転軌道にさまよっている小さな塵です。③小さなもので直径0.1ミリメートルくらい、大きなものでも直径数センチメートルだといわれています。④これが地球の大気圏に突入するときに燃え、明るい光を放つのです。

⑤流星のもとになる塵は、主に彗星が残していったものです。⑥彗星は、たくさんの塵を含んだ氷の塊のようなものです。⑦太陽から離れた場所にいるときは凍りついています。⑧太陽に近づくにつれ氷が融け、さまざまな物質を残していきます。⑨彗星が通過したあとに飛行機雲のように残る物質は、ダストトレイルと呼ばれます。

⑩地球が、公転軌道上に残されたダストトレイルの中を通過すると、細かい塵が地球上に降り注ぎます。⑪このとき、地球上からは多くの流星が観測できるのです。

Why do stars shine?

①Of all the stars, the ones which give off light are called fixed stars. ②Fixed stars give off energy because of nuclear fusion reactions. ③Nuclear fusion reactions form four hydrogen atoms into one helium atom. ④This type of reaction is also applied to hydrogen bombs and it gives off a great deal of energy.

⑤The sun is one of the fixed stars. ⑥It is said that the temperature of the corona around the sun is more than one million degrees C. ⑦Fixed stars shine because they are heated to a high temperature and give off a great deal of energy such as light and heat energy.

⑧Some stars do not give off light. ⑨Examples of these are the planets going around a fixed star such as Jupiter, Venus, and the earth. ⑩Seen from the earth, these two stars appear to shine. ⑪However, these planets do not give off light but just reflect light from the sun, a fixed star.

第1章 宇宙の疑問

問12　なぜ、星は光るの？

答　①星の中でも自ら光を出している星は、恒星と呼ばれています。②恒星は、核融合によってエネルギーを放出しています。③核融合というのは、4個の水素原子が1個のヘリウム原子になる反応です。④これは水素爆弾に使われている反応で、非常に大きなエネルギーを発生します。

⑤太陽も恒星の一つです。⑥太陽を取り巻くコロナの温度は摂氏100万度以上もあるといわれています。⑦恒星が光るのは、このように核融合によって高温になり、大量の光や熱などのエネルギーを放出しているからです。

⑧自ら光を出さない星もあります。⑨たとえば、木星や金星、地球などのように、恒星の周りを回る惑星です。⑩地球から見ると、これらの2つの星も光り輝いているように見えます。⑪これらの惑星は実際に輝いているわけではなく、恒星である太陽の光を反射しているだけなのです。

太陽系の構成はこうなっている
This is how the solar system is made up.

太陽系
The solar system

ブラックホール
Black hole

太陽
Sun

隕石
Meteor

水星
Mercury

金星
Venus

彗星
Comet

地球
Earth

火星
Mars

木星
Jupiter

宇宙ロケット
Space rocket

土星
Saturn

天王星
Uranus

人工衛星
Satellite

海王星
Neptune

宇宙
Universe

Chapter 2

Questions about the earth

第2章
地球の疑問

Qustions and answers about science

Q13   Why does the sky look blue?

①Smoke is often used as a stage effect in a concert hall. ②When smoke fills the hall, you can see a spotlight, which you can not see in other ways, as a line of a color such that you can see a red spotlight as a red line. ③This is a phenomenon called scattering whereby light hits particles in the air and changes direction. ④By this scattering, light, which you can not see in other ways, comes to be seen as a color.

⑤The color of a visible light, a kind of electromagnetic wave, changes according to its wavelength. ⑥Light with a short wavelength looks blue and light with a longer wavelength looks yellow or red. ⑦Scattering changes according to the wavelength of light and the size of the particles in the air. ⑧Smoke on the stage scatters all the colors of light such as red, blue, and yellow because the particles of the smoke are big. ⑨Small particles are likely to scatter blue light, which has a short wavelength.

第2章　地球の疑問

⑩There are molecules of oxygen and nitrogen in the thick
　　　　　モラキュールズ
　　　　　分子　　　　　酸素　　　　窒素　　　　　　厚い大気の層

layer of atmosphere covering the earth and they scatter
　　　　　　　　　　　～を覆っている—

sunlight. ⑪They are likely to scatter blue light but do not
太陽の光

scatter much red and yellow light because the molecules of

gas in the air are small. ⑫The sky looks blue because blue
気体　　　　　　　　　　　　　　　　　～に見える

light in sunlight is scattered in the air. (see p.54)

問⑬　　　　空はどうして青いの？

答 ①コンサート会場の演出で、スモークが使われることがあります。②煙が会場に充満すると、それまで見えなかったスポットライトの光が、赤い光は赤い線になってというように、色の線として見えるようになります。③これは、小さな粒にぶつかった光が方向を変える「散乱」と呼ばれる現象です。④散乱によって、それまで見えなかった光が「色」として見えるようになるのです。⑤電磁波である可視光線の色は、その波長によって変わります。⑥波長が短い光は、私たちに青く見え、波長が長くなると黄色や赤に見えます。⑦散乱は、光の波長と散乱する「粒」の大きさに関係します。⑧ステージのスモークが赤、青、黄色、すべての光を散乱するのは、煙の粒が大きいからです。⑨小さな粒だと、波長が短い青い光ほど散乱します。⑩地球をとり囲む厚い大気の層には酸素や窒素の分子があり、これらが太陽の光を散乱します。⑪気体の分子は小さいので、青い光を多く散乱し、赤や黄色の光はほとんど散乱しません。⑫空が青く見えるのは、太陽光の中の青い光が空で散乱しているからなのです。

43

Q14   Why are sunsets red?

①The atmosphere of the earth is more than 500
大気圏
kilometers thick. ②There are big particles such as
500キロメートルの厚さ　　　　　　　　　　　粒
water vapor and dust in the low layer of the atmosphere
水蒸気　　　　塵　　低層
from the surface of the earth to 35 kilometers high. ③It was
地表から高度35キロメートルまでの
mentioned on pp. 42-43 that blue light in sunlight is likely
〜で述べられた　　　　　　　　　　　　太陽光　　　〜しやすい
to be scattered by small particles such as molecules of
〜によって散乱される　　　　　　　　　　　　　分子
oxygen and nitrogen. ④On the other hand, bigger particles
酸素　　　窒素　　　　一方
such as water vapor and dust scatter red and yellow light.

⑤In the evening, sunlight travels a long distance in the air
　　　　　　　　　　　　　進む　　長い距離
along the surface of the earth and reaches your eyes. ⑥As
　　　　　　　　　　　　　　　　　〜に届く
this happens, blue light is scattered and little of it can reach
これが起きている間に　　　　　　　　　　　　それはほとんど〜できない
your eyes. ⑦However, sunlight in the evening looks reddish
　　　　　　　　　　　　　　　　　　　　　　　　　　　　　　　　　　赤っぽい
because red light travels through the air with little
　　　　　　　　　　　　　　　　　　　　　　　　　　　　　　　ほとんど散乱せずに
scattering.

⑧The sky in the west becomes red when this red light is

scattered by big particles such as water vapor and dust.

⑨This is what red sunsets are. (see p.54)
　　　　夕焼けがそうであるところのもの

44

第2章 地球の疑問

問14　夕焼けはなぜ、赤いの？

答 ①地球の大気圏は500キロメートル以上の厚さがあります。②そのうち、地表から高度35キロメートルまでの低層には水蒸気や塵など、大きな粒が多く漂っています。③太陽光の中の青い光は、大気中の酸素や窒素の分子など、小さな粒によって散乱しやすいことは、42〜43ページで説明したとおりです。④一方、水蒸気や塵など比較的大きな粒は、赤や黄色の光を散乱します。

⑤夕方になると、太陽の光は地表に沿うように、長い距離、大気の中を通過して私たちの目に届きます。⑥その間に、青い光は散乱して少なくなってしまいます。⑦一方、赤い光は、ほとんど散乱することなく大気を突き抜けるので、夕方の太陽光は赤っぽく見えます。

⑧この赤っぽい光を、水蒸気や塵など、大きな粒が散乱すると、空が赤く染まったように見えます。⑨これが夕焼けの正体です。

Why is seawater salty?

①There was no sea on the earth four billion years ago. ②At that time, the earth was extremely hot and water was held in the atmosphere in a state of vapor. ③It is thought that the atmosphere contained hydrogen chloride besides water vapor, carbon dioxide, nitrogen, and so on.

④After the earth cooled down in the course of time, it started raining. ⑤It was the rain of hydrochloric acid, that is hydrogen chloride in water. ⑥This rain of hydrochloric acid fell to the ground, dissolved various substances, and made pools in hollow places. ⑦This is how seas were born.

⑧Newborn seawater was not salty like it is today, but it was sour because it was hydrogen chloride water. ⑨The hydrogen chloride vaporized and fell to the ground as rain again and again. ⑩During that time, hydrogen chloride water dissolved a large amount of sodium and magnesium

第2章　地球の疑問

on the sea bottom and on the ground. ⑪As a result, sodium
　　　海底　　　　　　　　　　　　　　　　塩化ナトリウム

chloride and magnesium chloride were formed in a
　　　　　　塩化マグネシウム　　　　　　生成された

chemical reaction and accumulated in the sea. ⑫This is
化学反応によって　　　　　　　〜に蓄積された

how the sour seawater of the old days became salty as it is
　　　　　　　　　　　　　大昔の

today.

問15　海水はなぜ、塩辛いの？

答　①今から40億年以上前、地球に海はありませんでした。②非常に高温だったため、水分は水蒸気の状態で大気に含まれていました。③当時の大気は、水蒸気、二酸化炭素、窒素などのほかに、塩化水素を含んでいたと考えられています。

④時間がたつにつれて地球の温度が下がると、雨が降るようになりました。⑤雨といっても、水に塩化水素が溶けた塩酸の雨です。⑥塩酸の雨は地表にある物質を溶かしながら流れ、くぼんだ場所にたまりました。⑦これが海の誕生です。

⑧生まれたばかりの海の水は、今のように塩辛くなく、酸っぱい塩酸でした。⑨塩酸は蒸発して、再び雨となり地上に降り注ぐことを繰り返しました。⑩その過程で、塩酸が海底や地表のナトリウムやマグネシウムなどを大量に溶かし出しました。⑪これが化学反応によって塩化ナトリウムや塩化マグネシウムとなり、海に蓄積されていきました。⑫こうして酸っぱかった海の水が、今のように塩辛くなったのです。

Why is a mountain top colder though it is nearer to the sun?

①It is said that every 100 meters higher you go the temperature falls by about 0.6 degrees Celsius. ②You must wonder why high places are colder though they are nearer to the sun.

③Even the highest mountain is not more than 9,000 meters high. ④This distance is nothing compared with the distance between the sun and the earth, about 150 million kilometers. ⑤Therefore the height of mountains has nothing to do with the differences in temperature.

⑥The reason why higher places are colder has something to do with air convection and air pressure. ⑦At first, the ground is heated by the sun, and then the air near the ground is heated by the infrared light given off by the ground. ⑧Heated air goes up because it is light. ⑨Only this must make you think that higher places are warmer. ⑩The reason why mountain tops are colder is that the air pressure

第2章　地球の疑問

is lower at higher places. ⑪Heated air expands as it goes to
　　　　　　　より低い　　　　　　　　　　　膨らむ　　　～するにつれて
higher places, where the air pressure is lower. ⑫An

adiabatic expansion happens as air expands. ⑬It is the
断熱膨張　　　　　　　　　　　　～する過程で
phenomenon by which temperature falls when air expands
現象　　　　それによって～するところの
rapidly. ⑭Higher places are colder because of this adiabatic
急速に
expansion.

問16　山の上は太陽に近いのに、どうして寒いの？

答　①標高が 100 メートル高くなるごとに、気温は摂氏約
0.6 度下がるといわれています。②「高いほうが太陽に近いの
に、どうして寒くなるの？」と、疑問に思うでしょう。
③高いといっても、一番高い山でも 9000 メートル以下。④太
陽と地球の距離、約 1 億 5000 万キロメートルに比べれば、
この差はごくわずかです。⑤これでは気温に影響しません。
⑥標高が高くなると気温が下がる理由は、空気の対流と気圧に
関係します。⑦まず、太陽の熱によって地面が温められ、地面
から放たれる赤外線によって、地面付近の空気が温められます。
⑧温められた空気は軽くなるため、上昇します。⑨これだけなら、
上に行くに従って気温が上がるはずです。⑩山の上のほうが気
温が低いのは、標高が高くなるに従って気圧が低くなるからで
す。⑪暖かい空気のかたまりは、気圧が低い上空に行くにつれ
て膨らみます。⑫その過程で、断熱膨張という現象が起こります。
⑬気体が急激に膨張すると、温度が下がる現象です。⑭この断
熱膨張によって、高度が上がるにつれ気温が下がるのです。

49

Q17　How are auroras formed?

①The sun keeps giving off plasma. ②Plasma is a
stream of particles which have a positive or a
negative electric charge. ③It is sometimes called the solar
wind because it moves like a wind and covers the solar
system.

④The earth is a huge magnetic body and is surrounded by
a magnetic field, whose south pole is around the Arctic
Zone and whose north pole is around the Antarctic Zone.
⑤The earth's magnetic field is stretched widely in the
opposite direction to the sun by the solar wind. ⑥The sun
has a magnetic field, too. ⑦The sun's magnetic field is
strong enough to cover the earth's magnetic field.
⑧Magnetic fields have the property of keeping plasma
away. ⑨However, when the sun's magnetic field touches the
earth's magnetic field, plasma enters the earth's magnetic
field and rushes into the earth's Arctic Zone and Antarctic
Zone along the earth's magnetic field lines with a great deal

50

第2章　地球の疑問

of energy. ⑩At that time, plasma collides with atoms and
　　　　　　　　　　　　　　　衝突する　　　　　　原子
molecules of oxygen and nitrogen in the upper atmosphere
分子　　　　酸素　　　　窒素　　　　高層大気
and light-emitting phenomena take place. ⑪This is how
　　　　光を放つ〜　　　現象　　　起こる
auroras are formed. (see p.55)
オーロラのでき方

問17　　オーロラはどうやってできるの？

答　①太陽は、いつもプラズマを放出しています。②プラズ
マとは、正または負の電荷をもった粒子の集まりです。③風の
ように流れて太陽系を覆っていることから、太陽風とも呼ばれ
ています。

④地球は北極付近をS極、南極付近をN極とする大きな磁石
のかたまりであり、磁場に囲まれています。⑤地球の磁場は、
太陽風の影響で太陽と反対方向に大きく引き伸ばされたような
形をしています。⑥太陽にも磁場があります。⑦これは非常に
強いもので、地球の磁場を覆っています。

⑧磁場はプラズマを寄せつけない性質があります。⑨しかし、
太陽の磁場と地球の磁場が接すると、プラズマは地球の磁場に
入り込み、大きなエネルギーを持ちながら地球の磁力線に沿っ
て北極や南極付近になだれ込みます。⑩このとき、プラズマが
高層大気中の酸素や窒素の原子・分子に衝突して光を放ちます。
⑪これがオーロラです。

Q18   Does air have weight?

①In daily life we do not feel the weight of air, but, in fact, it has weight. ②1,000 liters of air at 1 atmosphere weighs about 1.2 kilograms.

③The weight of air, 1.2 kilograms per 1,000 liters, is only a thousandth the weight of water, so you may think it is very light. ④However, you are on the ground, which is at the bottom of a thick layer of air. ⑤Air pressure is put on you on the ground just like the heavy water pressure that is put on you when you dive into the deep sea. ⑥To be exact, air weighs 1 kilogram per square centimeter and 10 tons per square meter. ⑦To put it simply, air weighs as much as the weight of 10 compact cars per square meter.

⑧It is not easy to weigh air on the earth. ⑨If you put 1,000 liters of air at 1 atmosphere in a bag and weigh it, it just weighs 0 grams. ⑩Since the weight of the air in the bag and the buoyancy of the air around it are in balance, nobody can detect the weight of the air.

第2章 地球の疑問

問18　空気に重さはあるの？

答　①私たちの日常生活の中で、空気の重さを感じることはありませんが、空気にも重さがあります。②1気圧の空気の重さは 1000 リットルで約 1.2 キログラムです。
③1000 リットルで 1.2 キログラムという空気の重さは水の 1000 分の 1 であり、大したことはないと思うかもしれません。④しかし、私たちがいる地上は厚い空気の層である大気の底です。⑤深海に潜るとすごい水圧がかかるように、地上にも空気の圧力がかかっています。⑥それがどのくらいかというと、1平方センチあたり 1 キロ、1 平方メートルで 10 トン。⑦つまり、1 平方メートルあたり小型乗用車 10 台分にも相当するのです。
⑧地球上で空気の重さを量ろうとしても簡単ではありません。⑨1 気圧の空気、1000 リットルを袋に入れて重さを量っても、0 グラムにしかなりません。⑩袋の中の空気の重さと周囲の空気の浮力とつり合ってしまうため、重さがないことになってしまうからです。

53

空の青も夕焼けの赤も、光の散乱による
The sky looks blue and sunset looks red because light is scattered.

青空
Blue sky

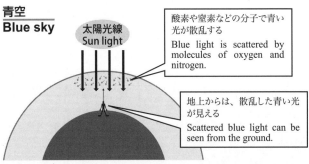

太陽光線
Sun light

酸素や窒素などの分子で青い光が散乱する

Blue light is scattered by molecules of oxygen and nitrogen.

地上からは、散乱した青い光が見える

Scattered blue light can be seen from the ground.

夕焼け
Sunset

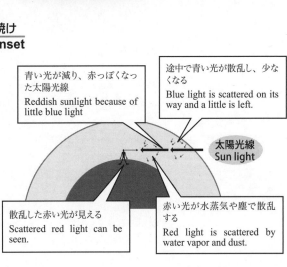

青い光が減り、赤っぽくなった太陽光線

Reddish sunlight because of little blue light

途中で青い光が散乱し、少なくなる

Blue light is scattered on its way and a little is left.

太陽光線
Sun light

散乱した赤い光が見える

Scattered red light can be seen.

赤い光が水蒸気や塵で散乱する

Red light is scattered by water vapor and dust.

オーロラとは、地球の地磁気に引き込まれた プラズマによる発光現象のこと

Auroras are formed by light-emitting phenomena with plasma pulled by the earth's geomagnetism.

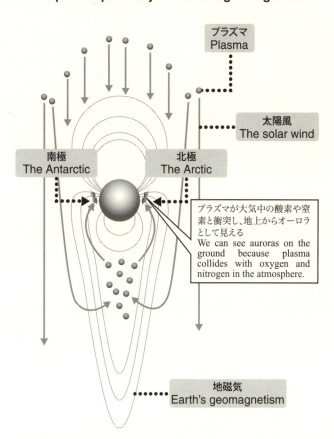

How do earthquakes happen?

①The central part of the earth is called the core and the part around it is called the mantle. ②Outside the mantle there is a layer of a few tens of kilometers thickness called the crust, covers the surface of the earth.

③The mantle is a layer of rocks from the inner surface of the crust to a depth of 2,900 kilometers. ④Although the outermost part of the mantle moves very slightly, the part from 100 to 400 kilometers deep of the mantle supposed to be moving slowly because of the heat convection. ⑤In other word, it seems like that masses of the outer mantle and the crust are floating on the layer moving with the convection.

⑥These floating parts are called plate. ⑦There are two kinds of plate; continental plates and oceanic plates. ⑧The surface of the earth is covered with more than ten plates.

⑨Scientists think that these plates are moved by the mantle's

第2章　地球の疑問

convection, and that they run into or overlap one another.
　　　　　　　　　　　～に衝突する　～に重なる　互いに
⑩When some plates move, a heavily loaded part may give
　　　　　　　　　　　　　大きく負荷のかかった部分　　　耐えられなくなる
way, cracking or sliding. ⑪This is how earthquakes happen.
　　　ひび割れる　ずれる
(see p.66)

問19　地震はどうして起きるの？

答　①地球の中心にはコア（核）と呼ばれる部分があり、その外側にマントルがあります。②さらにその外側には数十キロメートルの厚さの地殻があり、これが地球の表面を覆っています。③マントルは、地殻の下から深さ2900キロメートルまで続く岩石の層です。④最上部はほとんど動きませんが、深さ100〜400キロメートルの部分は、熱によりゆっくりと対流していると考えられています。⑤つまり、対流によって動く層の上に、マントルの最上部と地殻がかたまりとなり、浮いているような状態です。

⑥このかたまりはプレートと呼ばれています。⑦プレートには大陸プレートと海洋プレートがあります。⑧地球の表面は10数枚のプレートで覆われています。⑨これらはマントルの対流により移動し、ぶつかったり重なり合ったりしていると考えられています。⑩そして、プレートが移動して、ある部分に大きな力が加わり、耐えられなくなると、そこがひび割れたり、ずれたりします。⑪これが地震です。

57

How were the deserts formed?

①You may think of the deserts as sand areas from their Japanese name, *sabaku*. ②However, sand areas are called sandy deserts. There are also many rock deserts in the world, in which bare rocks are exposed. ③Deserts are formed under environments in which the amount of evaporation is greater than the rainfall. ④When the natural factor such as dry air or salt in the ground interrupt the growth of plants, the topsoil enriched with organic matters is washed away by the rain and blown away by the wind. ⑤This process finally makes the barren land where animals and plants can hardly survive. ⑥This is how the deserts are formed.

⑦The characteristic of a desert climate is the big difference in the temperature between day and night because it is dry. ⑧The surface temperature of rocks goes up in direct sunlight during the day and it goes down at night. ⑨In the course of this change of temperature, broken-up rocks are blown away or hit each other and become small pieces.

第2章　地球の疑問

⑩The sand made in this way is piled up to make a sandy
　　　　　　　　このようにして　積み重なって〜になる
desert.

問20　　砂漠はどうやってできたの？

答 ①「砂漠」というと、砂地だと思いがちです。②しかし、砂に覆われているのは砂砂漠であり、世界的に見て多いのは岩肌がむき出しになった岩石砂漠です。

③砂漠ができる原因となるのは、降水量よりも水の蒸発量が多い環境です。④乾燥や地表の塩分などにより植物が育ちにくくなると、有機物を含んだ表土が流されたり風に飛ばされたりしてなくなります。⑤その結果、さらに動植物が生息しにくい不毛の地と化してしまいます。⑥これが砂漠です。

⑦乾燥しているため、昼夜の気温の差が大きいことが砂漠の気候の特徴です。⑧昼間は直射日光を浴びた岩の表面温度は上昇し、夜になると冷えます。⑨これを繰り返しているうちに、岩はぼろぼろに崩れ、風に飛ばされたり、ぶつかり合ったりして細かくなります。⑩こうしてできた砂が堆積すると、砂砂漠になります。

Q21 Which is colder, the North Pole or the South Pole?

①You may think the North Pole and the South Pole are of the same temperature because they are both polar areas, but, in fact, the South Pole is colder.

②The South Pole is a continent and has various landform changes, as is the case with other continents. ③There are mountains such as the Ellsworth Mountains and the Yamato Mountains. ④The highest mountain is Vinson Massif, which is 4,892 meters above sea level and higher than the Matterhorn in the Alps.

⑤The North Pole is a sea covered with ice. ⑥The ice is about ten meters thick on average and there are no high places unlike the South Pole.

⑦In general, when you compare temperatures in places on the same latitude, land is likely to be colder than sea and highlands are likely to be colder than lowlands. ⑧The reason why the South Pole is colder is that it is land and is

第2章　地球の疑問

higher above sea level. ⑨It is said that the average
　　　　　　　　　　　　　　　　　　　　　　　平均気温
temperature at the South Pole is about 20 degrees C lower
　　　　　　　　　　　　　　　　　　　　　　　　　～よりも摂氏20度低い
than that at the North Pole. ⑩The lowest temperature
　　　　　　　　　　　　　　　　　　　　　　　最低気温
measured on earth is minus 89.2 degrees C, recorded at
～で観測された　　　　　摂氏マイナス89.2度　　　　　～で記録された
Vostok Station at the South Pole on July 21, 1983.
ボストーク基地

問21　北極と南極では、どちらが寒いの？

答　①北極と南極はどちらも極地であるため、気温も変らな
いように思うかもしれませんが、寒いのは南極のほうです。
②大陸である南極は、ほかの大陸と同じように地形の変化に富
んでいます。③エルスワース山脈、やまと山脈などの山脈が
あります。④最高峰であるヴィンソン・マシフ山は標高 4,892
メートルと、アルプスのマッターホルンをしのぎます。
⑤北極は、氷に覆われた海です。⑥氷の厚さは平均 10 メート
ルぐらいで、南極のように標高が高い場所がありません。
⑦一般的には、同緯度の場所を比較すると、海よりも陸、低地
よりも高地の気温が低くなる傾向があります。⑧南極が寒いの
も、陸地であり標高が高いという理由からです。⑨平均気温を
比較すると、南極のほうが北極より 20 度ほど低いとされてい
ます。⑩また、地球上で観測された最低気温は、1983 年 7 月
21 日に南極のボストーク基地で記録されたマイナス 89.2 度
です。

61

Why doesn't lake water soak into the bottom?

①The bottom of a lake is usually covered with pebbles, sand, and so on. ②However, a lake is always full of water. ③So, why doesn't lake water soak into the bottom of a lake?

④Since the bottom of a lake is covered with pebbles, sand, soil, and so on, water actually soaks into the bottom. ⑤However, there are always layers of rock or clay under the bottom and these layers do not take in much water. ⑥The water which soaks into the pebbles and sand piles up on these layers. ⑦After that, some of the water flows away as underground water.
⑧It is true that some water soaks into the bottom of a lake or evaporates from the surface of the lake, but it seems that lake water does not soak into the bottom of a lake because the same amount of water is added by rivers, rain, melted snow, and so on. (see p.67)

第2章 地球の疑問

問22　湖の水はどうして、底にしみ込まないの？

答　①湖の底は多くの場合、小石や砂などで覆われています。②にもかかわらず、湖はいつも水をたたえています。③なぜ、湖の水は湖底にしみ込まないのでしょうか？
④湖の底は、小石や砂、土などで覆われており、水がしみ込みます。⑤しかし、その下には必ず岩や粘土の層があり、ほとんど水を通しません。⑥湖の底の砂や小石にしみ込んだ水は、この層の上にたまります。⑦そして、その一部は地下水となって流出します。
⑧湖底にしみ込んだり、湖面から蒸発する水もありますが、流れ込む川や、雨、雪どけによって水が補給されるために、湖の底に水がしみ込んでいないように見えるのです。

Why are snow crystals hexagonal?

①There are various shapes of snow crystals but perfectly formed ones are all hexagonal. ②If you look closely, you will find that not only snow crystals but also ice crystals such as needle ice are hexagonal.

③A water molecule is made up of two hydrogen atoms and one oxygen atom. ④Two hydrogen atoms form an angle of 105 degrees. ⑤Because water molecules, composed of two atoms of hydrogen and one atom of oxygen, form three-dimensional and hexagonal ice crystals with angles of 105 degrees. ⑥Although each angles of the crystals are actually 105 degrees, regular hexagons with the angles of 120 degrees can be seen from a certain angle. ⑦This is the most stabilized state for mass of the water molecules.

⑧The snow is ice crystals: the water vapor three-dimen-

第2章　地球の疑問

sionally crystallized in the chilled air. ⑨The snow crystals
　　　　結晶化した　　　　　冷えた
are formed based on the regular hexagon. ⑩Though the
　　　　　　　　　　　　　　　　　　　　　　　　　　　～だが
crystals of the snow have a great variety in the
　　　　　　　　　　　　　　いろいろな種類
shapes, hexagons can be seen from a certain angle.

(see p.67)

問23　　　雪の結晶はなぜ、六角形なの？

答　①雪の結晶にはさまざまな形のものがありますが、美しく成長したものはすべて六角形です。②雪だけでなく、霜柱など氷の結晶を調べてみると、やはり六角形をしていることがわかります。

③水の分子は2個の水素原子と1個の酸素原子が結びついています。④2個の水素は、105度の角度を保っています。⑤1個の酸素原子と2個の水素原子でできた水の分子は、105度の角度のまま立体的な六方晶形の氷の結晶をつくるからです。⑥結晶のそれぞれの角は105度ですが、ある角度から見ると角が120度の正六角形に見えます。⑦これが水分子が集まって安定した状態です。

⑧雪は、水蒸気が冷たい空気中で立体的に結晶化したものです。⑨雪の結晶ができるときに基本となるのは、正六角形です。⑩雪の結晶にはいろいろな形がありますが、ある方向から見ると六角形に見えるのです。

地震の多くは、地球のプレートが ぶつかり合って起きる

Most earthquakes happen when plates in the earth run into one another.

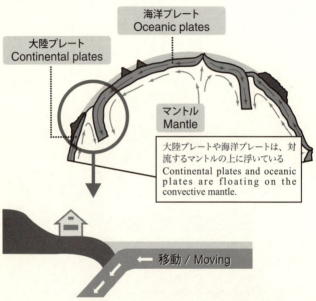

海洋プレート
Oceanic plates

大陸プレート
Continental plates

マントル
Mantle

大陸プレートや海洋プレートは、対流するマントルの上に浮いている
Continental plates and oceanic plates are floating on the convective mantle.

← 移動 / Moving

大陸プレートに海洋プレートが潜り込むところに大きな力が蓄積されると、地震が起きる

An earthquake happens because of a heavily loaded part in which an oceanic plate get under a continental plate may give way.

地震
Earthquake

湖の水がなくならないのは、湖底に水を通さない層があるから

A lake is always full of water because there are layers under the bottom and these layers do not take in water.

雨などで水分が補給される
Some water is added by rain and so on.

湖面から水分が蒸発する
Some water evaporates from the surface of the lake.

地下水として流出する
Some water flows away as underground water.

岩や粘度の層で保水する
Water is retained on the layers of rock or clay.

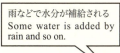

湖
Lake

岩や粘度の層
The layers of rock or clay

雪の結晶の形は、ある角度から六角形に見える

Snow crystals are seen regular hexagons from a certain angle

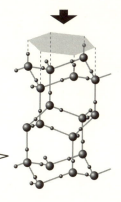

雪の結晶は複雑な形をしているが、ある角度から見ると正六角形に見える

Although a snow crystal has a complicated shape, you can find a regular hexagon when you see it from a certain angle.

Why does it snow though the temperature is not below 0 degrees C?

①Snow is ice crystals formed from water vapor:
high up in the sky, frozen water vapor forms ice
particles and they grow to form larger crystals as they fall.
②It snows when it is below 0 degrees C up in the air
regardless of the temperature on the ground. ③You may
think, "Why does not snow melt into rain as it falls when
the temperature on the ground is above 0 degrees C?"
④Even when it is warmer than 0 degrees C, it sometimes
snows without the snow melting. ⑤This is because snow
needs heat around it when it melts. ⑥Heat is needed to raise
the temperature of snow to 0 degrees C, the melting point
of ice. ⑦It needs more heat to melt snow. ⑧It needs as
much as about 80 kilocalories of heat per kilogram when
ice melts and turns into water. ⑨This amount of heat can
raise the same amount of water from 0 degrees C to 80
degrees C.

68

第2章　地球の疑問

⑩That is why snow stays on the ground without melting
　　そういうわけで　　　　　　地面に残る
even when you feel warm. ⑪For the same reason, snow
　　　　　　　　　　　　　　　同じ理由から
sometimes falls on the ground without melting in the air
even when the temperature is above 0 degrees C.

問24　気温が零度以下でなくても、なぜ雪が降るの？

答　①雪は、上空で水蒸気が冷やされてできた氷の粒が、落下中に成長して大きな結晶となったものです。②地上の気温に関係なく、上空が氷点下なら雪になります。③「地上の気温が0℃以上だったら、雪は空中で融けて雨になるのでは？」と思うでしょう。

④気温が0℃より高くても、雪が融けずに降ることがあります。⑤これは、雪が融けるとき、周囲の熱が必要だからです。⑥まず雪の温度を融点の0℃まで上昇させるために熱が必要です。⑦雪が融けるには、さらに熱が必要です。⑧氷が融けて水になるためには、1キログラムあたり約80キロカロリーもの熱が必要なのです。⑨これは同量の水を0℃から80℃まで温めることができるほどの熱量です。⑩ポカポカと暖かく感じても、積もった雪が融けずに残るのは、このような理由からです。⑪気温が0℃以上でも、雪が空中で融けることなく地上に達することがあるのも、同じ理由です。

世界地図をみてみよう
Let's see the world map.

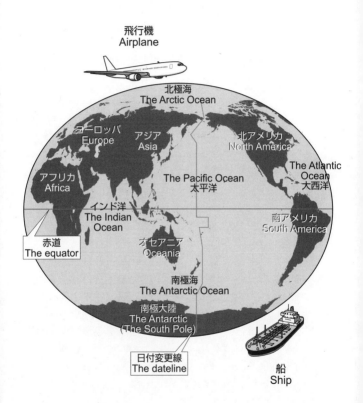

Chapter 3

Questions about creatures

第3章
生き物の疑問

Qustions and answers about science

Q25 Why did the dinosaurs die out?

①It is said that dinosaurs, which ruled the world for about 150 million years from over 200 million years ago, died out 65 million years ago at the end of the Mesozoic era in the Cretaceous period. ②There are various hypotheses about why they died out: attributing it to epidemic, a volcanic eruption, and so on. ③The most influential among them is a meteor strike.

④The basis for this hypothesis is a thin layer of metal, iridium, which covers the layer of the time when dinosaurs are thought to have died out. ⑤The iridium layer is found all over the world. ⑥Since there is almost no iridium on earth, it is thought that this metal was brought to earth by a meteor or something like that. ⑦Scientists say that a huge meteor, which struck the earth at the end of the Cretaceous period and made a crater of about 180 kilometers across on the Yucatan Peninsula, formed this layer.

⑧This huge meteor is about 10 kilometers across and, when it

第3章　生き物の疑問

struck the earth, it might have given off energy about 5 billion
　　　　　　　　　　　　　～を放出したかもしれない

times as much as the atomic bomb dropped over Hiroshima.
～の一倍の　　　　　　　原子爆弾　　　　　　～に投下された

⑨The most believable theory says that, because of this strike,
　　　　　　信ずべき

little sunlight reached the surface of the earth on account of
ほとんどない　　　　　　　　　表面　　　　　　　　　～のために

the great deal of dust with iridium which rose up, causing the
大量の粉塵　　　　　　　　　　　　　　　舞い上がった

whole earth to get colder and dinosaurs to die out.

問25　恐竜はなぜ、絶滅したの？

答 ①2億年以上前から約1億5000万年間、地球を支配したとされる恐竜が絶滅したのは、今から約6500万年前にあたる中生代白亜紀の末期だといわれています。②その理由については、伝染病説、火山の爆発などさまざまな説があります。③そのなかでも有力視されているのが、隕石衝突説です。

④その根拠となるのは、恐竜が絶滅したと思われる時代の地層を覆う、イリジウムという金属の薄い層です。⑤これは世界各地で発見されています。⑥イリジウムは、地球にはほとんど存在しないため、隕石などによって宇宙からもたらされたと考えられます。⑦イリジウムの層をつくったのは、白亜紀末期に地球に衝突し、ユカタン半島に直径約180キロメートルのクレーターをつくった巨大隕石だと考えられています。

⑧この巨大隕石は直径約10キロメートルほどもあり、衝突時のエネルギーは、広島型原爆の約50億倍と推定されています。⑨衝突により、イリジウムを含む大量の粉塵が舞い上がって地表に届く太陽光線が減少した結果、地球全体が寒冷化し、恐竜が絶滅したという説が有力です。

Q26 Why do animals have two sexes, male and female?

①Some species have one sex but can reproduce themselves. ②One example of this is potatoes in the ground. ③Although potato plants produce flowers and fruits, the potato, a part of the underground stem, is produced without pollination. ④If you put a potato in the ground, it will put out buds and its "child" grows up. ⑤A "child" reproduced without pollination in this way is a clone which has the same genes as its "parent". ⑥This means, if the "parent" is sensitive to the cold, the "child" is also sensitive to the cold.

⑦Mammals such as human beings reproduce themselves with fertilization, in which the female's egg nucleus and the male's sperm nucleus unite, and the child gets two halves of the genes which each of the parents has. ⑧In this case, even if the child's father is sensitive to the cold, the child is not always sensitive to the cold. ⑨Mammals can

第3章　生き物の疑問

have various children because of the combination of the
　　　　 さまざまな　　　　　　　　　　 組み合わせ
male's and the female's genes. ⑩A child of parents who are
　　　　　　　　　　　　　　　　　　　　　　　　　　　 ──
likely to be infected by a certain virus is sometimes not
 ～しやすい　 ～に感染する　　　 特定のウィルス
likely to be infected by the virus.

問26　動物はなぜ、雄と雌に分かれているの？

答　①生物の中には、雄と雌がいなくても子孫を増やせる種もあります。②たとえば、土の中にできるジャガイモです。③ジャガイモには花が咲き実もできますが、ジャガイモのいもは地下茎の一部であり、受精とはまったく関係なくできます。④これを土に埋めておけば、芽が出て「子」が育ちます。⑤このように、受精なしにできた子は、親とまったく同じ遺伝子を持つクローンです。⑥つまり、親が寒さに弱い個体だとすると、子も寒さに弱くなります。

⑦人間をはじめとする哺乳類のように、雌の卵の核と雄の精子の核とが合体する受精によって子ができる場合には、子は両親の遺伝子を半分ずつ受け継ぎます。⑧この場合、父親が寒さに弱いとしても、母親の遺伝子も受け継いでいる子は寒さに弱くなるとは限りません。⑨雄と雌の遺伝子の組み合わせにより多様な子孫を残せるのです。⑩同様に、特定のウィルスに感染しやすい個体の子孫が、同じウィルスに感染しにくくなることもあります。

75

Why Can Sparrows perch on Electric Wires?

①You can sometimes see sparrows or crows perched on the stripped overhead wires of the railroad. ②Why don't they get an electric shock?

③Electric shock occurs when an electric current flows through the body. ④An electric current flows through the body when each of the two points on the body touches two things which have different voltages. ⑤Birds perch on one electric wire with both legs. ⑥Even if 1,000 volts are applied to this electric wire, they do not get an electric shock because both of their legs are touching the electric wire.

⑦You are in danger of getting an electric shock when you fly a kite and it gets caught on the overhead wires of the railroad. ⑧That's because the ground has 0 volts and the overhead wires of the railroad have 1,000 volts or something. ⑨An electric current flows through the kite line

第3章　生き物の疑問

to you, and then, to the ground because these two points have different voltages. (see p.80)

問27　スズメはなぜ、電線にとまっても平気なの？

答　①スズメやカラスは平気で電線がむき出しになった電車の架線（かせん）などにとまっていることがあります。②なぜ、感電しないのでしょうか。

③感電とは、体に電流が流れて衝撃を受けることをいいます。④体に電流が流れるのは、電圧に差がある二つのものを体の2点で触れたときです。⑤鳥は一本の電線に両足をそろえてとまります。⑥その電線がたとえ1000ボルトだとしても、両足ともに1000ボルトに触れていることになり、感電しません。

⑦凧（たこ）あげをしているとき、凧が電車の架線にひっかかった場合などは、感電する危険があります。⑧架線の電圧が1000ボルトだとして、地面は常に0ボルトです。⑨2点に電圧の差があるため、凧糸—人間—地面と電流が流れるからです。

77

Q28 Why do migratory birds fly in a V-formation?

①Migratory birds move their wings up and down when they fly. ②When they lower their wings, the air pressure under the wings becomes higher than that of above them and this provides lifting power. ③This lifting power make birds fly in the sky.

④When birds move their wings, the flow of air changes around the tip of the wings. ⑤This is because some of the air pushed down by the wings goes up around the wings at both tips of the wings. ⑥This flow of air makes two vortexes behind each wing of the flying bird. ⑦These are called wing-tip vortexes in aeronautics.

⑧Air goes up in some parts of this flow of air and goes down in other parts of this flow of air making vortexes. ⑨A bird flying behind the bird making vortexes finds it easy to fly on the ascending air of the air flow.

⑩Therefore migratory birds fly in a V-formation because

第3章　生き物の疑問

the birds are following the ascending air of the wing-tip
〜のあとを追っている
vortexes made by the bird flying ahead of them. (see p.81)
〜の前を飛んでいる—

問28　渡り鳥はどうして、Ｖの字になって飛ぶの？

答　①渡り鳥が飛んでいるときには、翼を上下に動かしています。②翼を下げたとき、翼の下の気圧が上の気圧よりも高くなり、揚力が発生します。③この揚力によって、鳥は空を飛ぶことができるのです。

④鳥が翼を動かすと、翼の先のほうだけは空気の流れが変わります。⑤翼の下に押し下げられた空気が、両翼の先端で上に回り込んでしまうからです。⑥この空気の流れは、飛んでいる鳥の後方で両翼分の２本の渦となります。⑦航空用語でいう翼端渦です。

⑧この空気の流れは渦を巻いていますから、空気が上昇しているところと下降するところがあります。⑨後続の鳥は、空気が上昇しているところを飛べば、楽に飛べるわけです。

⑩つまり、渡り鳥がＶ字編隊になるのは、すぐ前の鳥が残した翼端渦が上昇している部分を追って後続する鳥が飛んでいるからです。

両足の間に電圧差がなければ、鳥は感電しない

Birds do not get an electric shock if they touch, with both legs, two points which have same voltage.

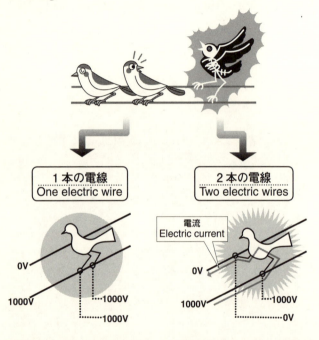

両足ともに 1000 ボルトであり、電圧に差がないため、電流が流れない

Its both legs touch the same voltage, 1000 volts, so no electric current flows through its body.

片足が 0 ボルト、もう一方の足が 1000 ボルトなら、両足に 1000 ボルトの電圧差があるため、大きい電流が流れる

One of its legs touches 0 volt and the other touches 1000 volts, in which voltage difference are 1000 volts, so a large electric current flows through its body.

渡り鳥は、前の鳥が作った空気の渦の上を飛ぶのでV字になる

Migratory birds fly in a V-formation because a bird flies on the vortex made by the bird flying ahead of it.

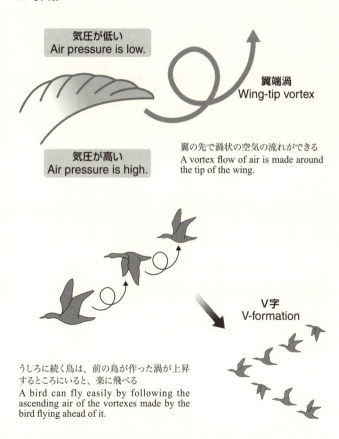

気圧が低い
Air pressure is low.

翼端渦
Wing-tip vortex

気圧が高い
Air pressure is high.

翼の先で渦状の空気の流れができる
A vortex flow of air is made around the tip of the wing.

V字
V-formation

うしろに続く鳥は、前の鳥が作った渦が上昇するところにいると、楽に飛べる
A bird can fly easily by following the ascending air of the vortexes made by the bird flying ahead of it.

Q29 Fish don't close their eyes but don't they sleep?

①Some fish such as gray shark or goggle-eyed
　　　　　　　　　　　　メジロザメ　　　ムツゴロウ
gobies have a membrane in their eyes, which
　　　　　　メムブレイン
　　　　　　　膜
takes the place of eyelids. ②Sunfish have muscles around
〜の代わりをする　まぶた　　マンボウ　　　　筋肉
the eye and they cover the eye, so they sometimes look as if

they are blinking. ③However, most of fish do not have
まばたきしているかのように見える
eyelids and they keep their eyes open. ④You may think that
　　　　　　　眼を開け続ける
fish do not sleep because they keep their eyes open, but

every fish does sleep.
　　　　　実際には眠る
⑤The time and place of sleeping depend on the kind of fish.
　　　　　　　　　　　　　　　　　〜による　〜の種類
⑥Flounders, right-eyed flounders, and congers, which are
　ヒラメ　　　カレイ　　　　　　　　アナゴ
active at night, sleep during the day, and parrot bass,
活発な　　　　　　　　　　　　　　　　　　　イシダイ
filefish, and rockfish sleep at the night.
カワハギ　　メバル
⑦The place of sleeping depends on the kind of fish, but

they all sleep in a place which is safe from attack such as
　　　　　　　　　　　　　　　　攻撃に対して安全な
space between rocks or in the sand.
岩の間や砂の中といった〜
⑧Migratory fish like tuna are always swimming, so they
　回遊魚　　　　　マグロ

82

第3章　生き物の疑問

sleep while swimming. ⑨However, if they fell fast asleep,
熟睡するなら
they would not be able to swim. ⑩They are swimming
泳ぐことができないだろう
while sleeping lightly.
浅く

問29　魚は眼を閉じないけれど、寝ないの？

答 ①メジロザメ、ムツゴロウなど一部の魚は、まぶたの役割をする膜を持ちます。②マンボウは眼の周囲の筋肉が眼を覆い、まばたきしているように見えることがあります。③しかし、ほとんどの魚にはまぶたがなく、いつも眼を開けています。④眠っているときも眼を開けているため、眠らないように見えますが、どんな魚も必ず眠ります。

⑤眠る時間や場所は、種類によって異なります。⑥夜行性のヒラメ、カレイ、アナゴなどは昼間に眠り、イシダイ、カワハギ、メバルなどは夜眠ります。

⑦眠る場所も魚の種類によって違い、岩の間や砂の中など敵に攻撃されにくい場所です。

⑧マグロのように、常に泳ぎ続けている回遊魚は、泳ぎながら眠ります。⑨といっても、完全に眠ってしまうと泳ぎ続けることなどできないはずです。⑩半分眠ったうとうと状態で眠りながら泳いでいるのです。

Q30 Why can salmon live both in the sea and the rivers?

①The important difference between fresh water and salt water for fish is osmotic pressure. ②Water flows from water with low osmotic pressure to that with high osmotic pressure. ③The osmotic pressure of seawater is higher than that of fresh water. ④The osmotic pressure of the body fluid of fresh water fish and seawater fish is almost the same; the pressure is just between that of seawater and fresh water. ⑤Therefore, even when fresh water fish are in fresh water, they are in danger of swelling up because their body takes in water. ⑥In contrast, even when seawater fish are in salt water, they are in danger of shedding too much water. ⑦It is the osmotic pressure adjustment function that controls this. ⑧Fresh water fish reduce the amount of water in their bodies by urinating a lot. ⑨On the contrary, seawater fish try not to urinate a lot and, at the same time, they give off salt through their gills.

⑩Fish which move from the sea to the rivers and from the

第3章　生き物の疑問

rivers to the sea such as salmon and eel are called
　　　　　　　　　　　　　サケ　　　　　ウナギ
euryhaline fish. ⑪Euryhaline fish have an osmotic pressure
広塩性魚
adjustment function which allows them to live both in the
　　　　　　　　　　　　　　～に—させる
sea and in rivers and can use it well in both types of water.

⑫Therefore they can live both in the sea and in rivers.

(see p.90)

問30　サケはどうして、海と川の両方で生きていけるの？

答　①魚にとって、淡水と塩水の大きな違いは浸透圧です。②水分は浸透圧が低いほうから高いほうへと移動します。③海水と淡水を比べると、浸透圧が高いのは海水です。④淡水魚と海水魚の体液の浸透圧はほぼ同じで、海水と淡水の中間の浸透圧です。⑤これが原因で、淡水魚は淡水中にいるとき、体が水を吸収し水ぶくれ状態になる危険にさらされています。⑥逆に、海水魚は塩水中にいると、水分が流出してしまう危険があります。⑦これを調整するのが、浸透圧調整機能です。⑧淡水魚は尿として多くの水分を排出し、体内の水分を減らします。⑨海水魚は逆に水分をあまり出さないようにすると同時に、エラから塩分を排出しています。

⑩サケやウナギのように川から海へ、海から川へと回遊する魚は、広塩性魚と呼ばれています。⑪広塩性魚は海水にも淡水にも対応する浸透圧調整機能を持ち、淡水と海水でこれを使い分けることができます。⑫そのため、川でも海でも生きていけるのです。

Q31 Don't lions become sick though they eat only meat, not vegetables?

①It is said that people who eat only meat are
likely to suffer from lifestyle diseases. ②Now,
you may wonder if meat-eating animals such as lions are
healthy.
③It is known that animals in the cat family such as lions
especially eat only meat. ④The members of the cat family
have a body system which keeps them healthy through
eating only meat. ⑤One of the reasons lies in
L-gulonolactone oxidase. ⑥Since the meat-eating animals
such as the members of the cat family have this oxidase,
they can make Vitamin C from grape sugar in their bodies.
⑦The nutrients they can't make in their bodies such as
Vitamin A are taken in by eating grass-eating animals.
⑧The meat-eating animals take in vitamins through eating
grass-eating animal's livers.
⑨Properly digested plants staying in the stomach and the

86

第3章　生き物の疑問

intestine of the grass-eating animals are also important

source of vitamins for them.
ビタミン源

問31　**ライオンは肉ばかり食べて野菜を
食べなくても、病気にならないの？**

答　①人間は、肉ばかり食べていると生活習慣病にかかりやすくなるといわれています。②そこで気になるのが、ライオンなどのように肉ばかり食べている肉食獣の健康です。③ライオンなどの猫科の動物は、特に強い肉食性を持っていることが知られています。④猫科の動物は、肉ばかり食べていても健康を保てるような体のしくみを持っているのです。⑤その一例がL-グロノラクトン酸化酵素です。⑥猫科をはじめとする肉食獣はこの酵素を持っているため、体内でブドウ糖からビタミンCを合成することができます。⑦ビタミンAなどの体内で合成できないものは、草食動物を食べることによって補います。⑧肉食動物は草食動物の肝臓を食べることによって、ビタミンを摂取します。
⑨草食動物や肉食動物の胃や小腸にある、適度に消化された植物も重要なビタミン源です。

87

Why do sunflowers always face to the sun?

①It is only growing sunflowers that follows the direction of the sun. ②Sunflowers which are in their growth period and have not started to bloom yet, face the sky at night, face east in the morning, and turn their faces from east to west to follow the sun in the daytime. ③This is the movement of the plants by a nature named phototropism.

④Phototropism of plants such as that of sunflowers is the nature caused by a kind of growth hormones named auxin. ⑤When this hormone reaches an amount, the plant speeds up its growth.
⑥The reason why the plants face to the sun is that the auxin moves to the side of their stem which does not catch sunlight. ⑦As a result, the amount of auxin is small on the side of the stem which catches sunlight and the amount of it on the side of the stem which does not catch sunlight is

第3章 生き物の疑問

good enough to grow up. ⑧The head of sunflower faces to
～するのに十分な
the sun because only the side of the stem which does not

catch sunlight speeds up its growth thanks to the difference
                                    ～のために　～の違い
in the amount of auxin between those sides.

問32 **ヒマワリの花はどうして、太陽のほうを
むいているの？**

答 ①花が太陽の方向を追うように動くのは、成長期のヒマワリだけです。②花が咲く前の成長期のヒマワリは、夜は上をむき、朝になると東をむき、日中は太陽の移動に合わせて南から西の方向に頭を回転させます。③これは、植物の屈光性（くっこうせい）と呼ばれる動きの一つです。

④ヒマワリをはじめとする植物の屈光性は、オーキシンと呼ばれる成長ホルモンの一種によるものです。⑤これが適度な濃度になると、植物は成長を早めます。

⑥植物が太陽の方向をむくのは、オーキシンが茎の中で光が当たらない方向に移動するからです。⑦その結果、茎の光が当たっている側のオーキシン濃度は低く、光があたらない側で成長に適した濃度になります。⑧ヒマワリの花が太陽の方向をむくのは、オーキシンの濃度差により、光が当たらない側だけ成長が早まるからです。

89

サケは、海水中と淡水中で、体内の水分と塩分を調整する
Salmons can control water and salt in them both in fresh water and in salt water.

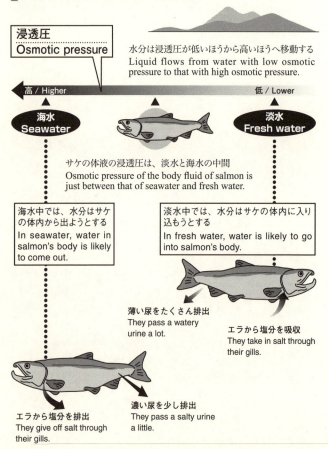

浸透圧
Osmotic pressure

水分は浸透圧が低いほうから高いほうへ移動する
Liquid flows from water with low osmotic pressure to that with high osmotic pressure.

高 / Higher　　　　　　　　　　　　　　　低 / Lower

海水
Seawater

淡水
Fresh water

サケの体液の浸透圧は、淡水と海水の中間
Osmotic pressure of the body fluid of salmon is just between that of seawater and fresh water.

海水中では、水分はサケの体内から出ようとする
In seawater, water in salmon's body is likely to come out.

淡水中では、水分はサケの体内に入り込もうとする
In fresh water, water is likely to go into salmon's body.

薄い尿をたくさん排出
They pass a watery urine a lot.

エラから塩分を吸収
They take in salt through their gills.

エラから塩分を排出
They give off salt through their gills.

濃い尿を少し排出
They pass a salty urine a little.

90

ひまわりの茎は、日陰側が活発に成長する
The side of the sunflowers' stem which does not catch sunlight grows well.

植物の成長ホルモンであるオーキシンは、太陽光が当たらない部分に移動する。
Auxin, a kind of plant growth hormone, moves to the part which does not catch sunlight.

日陰
Shade

日なた
Sunshine

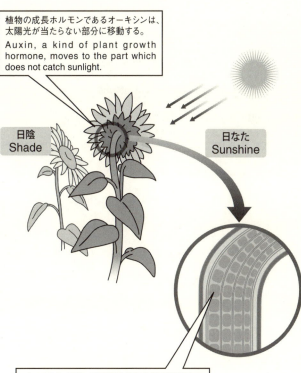

オーキシンが多い日陰側は細胞分裂が活発なので、成長が早い。
The side of the sunflowers' stem which does not catch sunlight and has much auxin grows fast because it undergoes cell division actively.

Q33 Why don't penguins live in the North Pole?

①You will probably be surprised to hear that penguins used to live at the North Pole. ②In fact, great auks living in the North Pole were commonly called "penguin" in the old days. ③Unfortunately, people hunted them too much and they died out in the 1840's. ④Around that time, Europeans often went to look around the southern hemisphere and they found a new kind of bird living around cold seaside in the southern hemisphere. ⑤Since the birds looked like the great auks, they came to be called penguin. ⑥They are the penguins we know today.

⑦Academically, these two kinds of birds are not closely related because great auks are Charadriiformes and penguins are Sphenisciformes. ⑧However, great auks were like penguins today.

⑨Both great auks and penguins could not cross the equator because they did not like heat. ⑩Scientists think that these

第3章　生き物の疑問

academically different birds became similar in the course
学術的に異なった　　　　　　　　　　　　　　　似た　　　進化の過程において
of evolution in a similar environment.
　　　似た環境のもとで

問33　ペンギンはどうして、北極にはいないの？

答　①「ペンギンは、もともと北極にいた鳥」だと聞くと、みなさんは驚くに違いありません。②実は「ペンギン」はもともと、北極にいたオオウミガラスにつけられた俗称でした。③残念なことに、この鳥は人間に乱獲され、1840年代に絶滅してしまいました。④ちょうどその頃、ヨーロッパ人による南半球の探検が盛んになり、南半球の寒い海辺に生息する新種の鳥が発見されました。⑤この鳥はオオウミガラスに似ていたためペンギンと呼ばれるようになりました。⑥これが現在のペンギンです。

⑦オオウミガラスはチドリ目であるのに対して、ペンギンはペンギン目であり、この2種類の鳥は分類上は近い仲間とはいえません。⑧にもかかわらず、オオウミガラスは現在のペンギンと同じような姿をした鳥でした。

⑨ペンギンもオオウミガラスも、暑さが苦手であるため赤道を横切って移動できなかったのでしょう。⑩その一方で、分類上まったく異なる鳥が似た環境のもとで進化するうちに、似た姿になったものと考えられています。

Q34   Why do ants walk in line?

①You sometimes see ants walking in line in parks or in your garden. ②The ants' line is sometimes more than 50 meters long. ③An ant follows the ant ahead of it even when they walk a long way. ④Ants walk in line mainly when they go out for food. ⑤When an ant finds food, it releases chemical substance from its body to make a trail and goes back to the nest with the food. ⑥This chemical substance, with which ants make a trail, is called pheromone. ⑦When the ant which has found food comes back to its nest, other ants in the nest start to go to the place where the food is following the trail pheromone. ⑧This forms the ants' line.
⑨Ants can do almost nothing with the help of their vision because their vision is very poor. ⑩Instead, they use their antennae to touch something and find out what it is, and also use pheromone as a means of sending messages.

(see p.100)

第3章　生き物の疑問

問34　アリはどうして、行列をつくって歩くの？

答　①公園や庭で、アリが行列をつくって歩いているところを見かけることがあります。②長さは時には50メートルを超えることもあります。③そんなに長い距離でも、後ろを歩くアリは前を歩くアリが歩いたあとをたどります。

④アリが行列をつくるのは、主に餌を探しに行くときです。⑤1匹のアリが餌を見つけると、腹部から目印になる物質を出しながら餌を抱えて巣に戻ります。⑥目印となるのは、フェロモンと呼ばれる物質です。⑦餌を見つけたアリが巣にたどり着くと、巣にいたアリたちは帰ってきたアリのフェロモンをたどり、餌の場所を目指します。⑧これがアリの行列です。

⑨アリは目がそれほど発達していないので、視覚に頼ることはほとんどできません。⑩それを補うのが、ものに触れて確認するための触角と、情報伝達の手段としてのフェロモンなのです。

Q35 Why aren't deep-sea fish crushed under water pressure?

①Fish living at a depth over 200 meters are generally called deep-sea fish. ②Water pressure at a depth of 200 meters is about 20 bar. ③An empty PET bottle (Polyethylene terephthalate bottle) with a cap sunk to this depth will be crushed flat under this pressure. ④Then, why aren't deep-sea fish crushed under such pressure? ⑤Fish living in shallow water such as horse mackerel and sardine have air bladders which enable them to rise and fall in the water according to the amount of air in them. ⑥The specific gravity of sea fish is higher than that of the seawater, so they can not come up without the air bladders. ⑦Then, what would happen if horse mackerel or sardine went down to the deep sea? ⑧They would die because their air bladders would be crushed. ⑨One of the reasons that deep-sea fish can live under high pressure lies in their air bladder. ⑩The air bladder of deep-sea fish is filled with fat,

第3章　生き物の疑問

and, in other points, they are also designed to live under
　　　そのほかの点において　　　　　　　　　～するように作られている
high pressure. ⑪Some deep-sea fish do not have an air

bladder. ⑫However, the secret of deep-sea fish is not well
　　　　　　　　　　　　　　　　　　　　　　　　　　　　　まだ～ない
understood yet. ⑬Their mysteries will be solved in the near
よく理解されていない　　　　　　　神秘　　　　　　解明される　　　近い将来
future.

問35　深海魚はなぜ、水圧に押しつぶされないの？

答　①深海魚とは、一般的に水深200メートル以下の深海に生息する魚を指します。②水深200メートルの水圧は約20気圧。③空のペットボトルにふたをして沈めると、ペシャンコになってしまうほどの力を受けます。④深海魚はこれだけの圧力を受けているにもかかわらず、なぜつぶれないのでしょうか？
⑤アジやイワシをはじめとした浅い海に暮らす魚は、空気の量で浮き沈みを調整するうきぶくろを持っています。⑥海水魚の比重は海水より重いため、うきぶくろがないと浮上することができません。⑦では、もしもアジやイワシが深海に行ったらどうなるでしょうか？⑧うきぶくろがつぶれて死んでしまうでしょう。⑨深海魚が強い水圧に耐えられる秘密の一つは、うきぶくろにあります。⑩深海魚のうきぶくろは、空気の代わりに脂肪で満たされるなど、高い水圧にも耐えられるような構造をしています。⑪なかには、うきぶくろを持たないものもいます。⑫ただし、深海魚についての研究はそれほど進んでいません。⑬今後、多くの謎が解き明かされることでしょう。

Q36 **Why do leaves turn red in autumn?**

①As the temperature falls, plants become inactive and the amount of water taken in from the roots becomes less. ②The trees die from lack of water if all the water taken in from the roots evaporates from the leaves. ③Therefore trees shed their leaves to avoid water evaporation and get ready for the cold season.

④A separation layer is formed between the leaves and the branch when the temperature starts falling. ⑤The leaves look green because they have the chlorophyll which is necessary for photosynthesis. ⑥The chlorophyll is broken down because the separation layer blocks the water and the nutrients.

⑦In the case of the plants, such as maple, whose leaves turn red, the separation layer blocks the flows of the sugar which is produced in the leaves and send to the branches.

⑧As the result, a red coloring matter called anthocyanin is made up from the sugar and it makes leaves turn red.

第3章　生き物の疑問

⑨The leaves such as of ginkgo turn yellow because they
　　　　　　　　　　イチョウ
have a yellow coloring matter called carotinoid.　⑩The
　　　　　　　　　　　　　　　　　　　カロテノイド
color of carotenoid, which is always in leaves, comes to

stand out as the chlorophyll is broken down.
目立つ

問36　秋になると、なぜ葉っぱが赤くなるの？

答　①温度が下がると植物の活動が鈍り、根が吸い上げる水の量が減ります。②もしも根が吸い上げた水分がすべて葉から蒸発してしまうと、水分が不足して、木は枯れてしまいます。③そこで木は、水分の蒸発を防ぐために葉を落として、寒い季節に備えます。④気温が下がり始めると、葉と枝の間に離層が形成されます。⑤木の葉が緑色に見えるのは、植物が光合成を行なうのに必要な葉緑素があるからです。⑥しかしながら、離層ができると，それが水分や養分の流れを妨げるため、この葉緑素が分解されていきます。

⑦モミジのように赤く色づく植物の場合、葉でつくられた糖分が離層によって枝に送られなくなります。⑧その結果、この糖分からアントシアニンという赤い色素が合成されて、木の葉は赤くなります。⑨イチョウなどで葉が黄色くなるのは、カロテノイドという黄色の色素によるものです。⑩カロテノイドはもともと葉に含まれていますが、葉緑素が分解されることにより、カロテノイドの黄色が目立ってくるわけです。

99

アリはほかのアリが出したフェロモンを目印にする
Ants follow the trail pheromone other ants release.

餌をみつける
Finding food

餌を見つけたアリは、腹部からフェロモンを出しながら巣に戻る
An ant which has found food comes back to its nest releasing a pheromone from its body.

巣にいたアリがフェロモンをたどり、餌集めに出発する
Ants in the nest start to go to the place in which there is food following the trail pheromone.

多くのアリがフェロモンをたどって餌集めに行くため、行列になる
A lot of ants go to get food following the pheromone and form the line.

木の葉が紅葉するのは、赤い色素ができるから
The leaves turn red because a red coloring matter is made.

木の葉が紅葉するしくみ
How the leaves turn red

①
葉緑素によりでんぷんが作られ、幹に送られている
Starch is made by chlorophyll and sent to the trunk.

②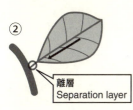

離層
Separation layer

寒くなると、葉緑素の働きが弱くなり、葉のつけ根に離層が形成される
Chlorophyll doesn't work well and a separation layer is formed at the root of a leaf when it becomes cold.

③
離層により幹に流れなくなった養分が葉にたまる。それが分解されて糖分になる
Nutrients stay in the leaves because the separation layer keeps them from entering the trunk. These nutrients are broken down into the sugar.

④
糖分から赤い色素であるアントシアニンが合成され、木の葉が赤く色づく
Anthocyanin, a red coloring matter, is made up from the sugar and the leaves turn red.

101

地球は生き物の宝庫です

There are many different creatures on the earth.

Chapter 4

Questions about human body

第4章

人間の体の疑問

Qustions and answers about science

Did human beings evolve from apes?

①Although all apes are grouped together, there is a bigger difference between chimpanzees and Japanese monkeys than between chimpanzees and human beings. ②It is chimpanzees that human beings are close to on the evolutionary tree. ③It is said that, about 5 million years ago, chimpanzees and human beings separated from a kind of ape which has died out, and each of them evolved differently. ④For a long time scientists could not find out what kind of ape the common ancestor of human beings and chimpanzees was. ⑤However, scientists today think that one of the anthropoids whose fossils have been found such as Nakalipithecus and Ouranopithecus, is the common ancestor of human beings and chimpanzees.

⑥In the study of genes, the difference between chimpanzees and human beings in DNA (deoxypentose nucleic acid) sequence is within several percentage points. ⑦This

第4章　人間の体の疑問

difference is very small in genetics. ⑧This small difference
                                 遺伝学
in genes is a result of the different evolutions for as long as 5
              結果   進化   ～もの
million years.

⑨Therefore it is wrong to say that human beings evolved

from apes. ⑩You should say that apes and human beings

have a common ancestor. (see p.116)

問37　ヒトはサルから進化したの？

答　①ひと言でサルといっても、チンパンジーとニホンザル
では、チンパンジーとヒト以上の違いがあります。②進化の系
統から見てヒトと近いのは、チンパンジーです。③チンパンジ
ーとヒトは、現在はいないサルと500万年ほど前に枝分かれ
し、ヒトとチンパンジーに分かれて進化したということです。
④ヒトとチンパンジーの共通の祖先がどのようなサルであった
のか、長い間わかりませんでした。⑤最近では、ナカリピテク
ス、オウラノピテクスなど、化石で発見された類人猿が、ヒト
とチンパンジー共通の祖先と考えられています。
⑥遺伝子の研究では、チンパンジーとヒトとのＤＮＡ配列の違
いは、数パーセント以内とされています。⑦この違いは、遺伝
学的に見るとほんのわずかにすぎません。⑧このわずかな遺伝
子の違いが500万年間にわたり、違う進化をしてきた結果な
のです。
⑨したがって、「ヒトはサルから進化」したというのは正しくあ
りません。⑩「サルとヒトの祖先は同じだ」というべきなのです。

Q38 Why must all human beings die?

①Some scientists say that telomere has something to do with the life span of human beings. ②Telomere is the tail-like part at the ends of chromosomes. ③Scientists say that telomere protects DNA, and that it is also necessary for cells to divide in order to make new normal cells.
④Most of the cells of living things divide to make new cells again and again. ⑤Telomeres shorten every time cells divide. ⑥When telomeres become short after cells divide a certain number of times, the cells stop dividing. ⑦It is thought that this is to prevent abnormal cell division such as cancer, which is caused by telomeres which are not sufficiently active. ⑧The state at which cells stop dividing is called cell aging.
⑨Today, it is said that the life span of human beings is about 120 years at longest. ⑩It is believed that telomere is one of the complicate factors which decide the life span

106

第4章　人間の体の疑問

of human beings.

問38　人間はなぜ、必ず死ぬの？

答　①人間の寿命にテロメアがかかわっている、という説があります。②テロメアというのは、染色体の両端にあるしっぽのような部分です。③このテロメアはDNAを守るだけでなく、正常に細胞分裂を行なうなどのために必要なものとされています。

④生物の多くの細胞は、分裂を繰り返しています。⑤テロメアは細胞分裂のたびに短くなっていきます。⑥そして、一定回数の細胞分裂を行ない、ある長さより短くなると、細胞は分裂をやめてしまいます。⑦これは、テロメアが十分に働かないことにより、癌化など、異常な細胞分裂を起こすことを防ぐためと考えられています。⑧細胞が分裂をやめたその状態が「細胞の老化」です。

⑨現在、人間の寿命は最長120歳前後とされています。⑩もちろん、人間の寿命を左右する要因は単純なものではありませんが、テロメアもその一つではないかと考えられています。

Q39 Why isn't the human body covered with hair like dogs or cats?

①There are some theories to explain why the human body is not covered with hair like most of the other mammals.
②One of them is the theory that human beings lost their hair to control their body temperature. ③When the ancestors of human beings lived in trees, they were not exposed to direct sunlight. ④Later, when they began to walk upright and live on grasslands, they had to work under the burning sun. ⑤The theory is that, in order to adapt themselves to these new surroundings, the sweat glands of human beings developed to control their body temperature by sweating and that they lost their hair at the same time.

⑥Another one is called "Human Neoteny Theory." ⑦Neoteny means that animals grow old with the characteristics they have at birth. ⑧Newborn chimpanzees have no hair. ⑨This theory is that human

108

第4章　人間の体の疑問

beings grow retaining the hairless feature of the juvenile
　　　　成長する　～をとどめたままで　無毛の　　特徴　　　幼年期
stage.

⑩There are other theories about this matter but none
　　　　　　　　　　　　　　　　　　　　この問題　　　　　～のどれも―ない
of them have been confirmed yet.
　　　　まだ確認されていない

問39　**ヒトはどうして、イヌやネコのように
全身が毛で覆われていないの？**

答　①ヒトがほかの哺乳類のように全身を体毛で覆われていない理由については、いくつかの説があります。

②まず、体温を調整するために、体毛を失ったとする説です。③ヒトの祖先が木の上で生活していたころには、直射日光にさらされることはありませんでした。④直立歩行を始め、草原で暮らすようになると、炎天下で活動しなければならなくなります。⑤この環境に合わせて、汗で体温調整ができるように汗腺を発達させ、同時に体毛を失ったとするものです。

⑥もう一つは、「人類ネオテニー説」と呼ばれるものです。⑦ネオテニーとは生まれたばかりの性質を残したまま成熟することです。⑧生まれたばかりのチンパンジーには体毛がありません。⑨ヒトは無毛という幼年期の特徴を備えたままで成長する生物だとするものです。

⑩ほかにも諸説ありますが、まだ定説とされるものはありません。

109

Why do you shed tears when you are sad?

①The surface of the eye is always covered with thin layer of tears. ②This is because tears reduce the effect of stimuli from outside and protect the eye. ③You shed tears when you have something in your eye and it's surface is stimulated. ④This is because the trifacial nerve is working.

⑤Tears which come in the eye when you are sad or happy are different from tears which come in the eye when it is stimulated. ⑥This is because the autonomous nerve is working. ⑦The autonomous nerve is made up of the sympathetic nerve and the parasympathetic nerve. ⑧When you are very much excited by anger or regret, the sympathetic nerve works actively and a small amount of salty tears comes in the eye. ⑨When you are sad or moved, the parasympathetic nerve works actively and a large amount of watery tears comes in the eye.

第4章　人間の体の疑問

⑩In tears, there are prolactin and adrenocorticotropic
　　　　　　　　　　プロラクチン　　　副腎皮質刺激ホルモン
hormones, which cause a state of tension under stress, and
　　　　　　　　　　　　～を引き起こす　緊張状態　　　ストレスにさらされて
manganese, a large amount of which is said to cause
マンガン　　　　　　　　　　　　　　　　　　　　　　～するといわれている
depression. ⑪Some scientists say that you feel good after you
うつ病
shed tears because these substances are passed out of the
　　　　　　　　　　　　　　　　　　　　　　～から排出される
body with tears.

| 問40 | なぜ、悲しいと涙が出るの？ |

答　①眼の表面にはいつも、少量の涙で覆われています。②眼が受ける刺激をやわらげ、眼を守るためです。③眼にごみが入ったときや、眼の表面が刺激を受けたときにも涙が出ます。④これらは三叉神経の働きによるものです。

⑤悲しいときやうれしいときなどに出る涙は、刺激を受けたときに出る涙とは違います。⑥それは自律神経によるものです。⑦自律神経は、交感神経と副交感神経に分かれています。⑧怒りや悔しさなどの強い感情の昂ぶりを感じたときには、交感神経のほうがよく働き、しょっぱい涙が少し出ます。⑨悲しいときや感動したときは、副交感神経のほうがよく働き、薄くて水っぽい涙が大量に出ます。

⑩涙にはプロラクチンや副腎皮質刺激ホルモンなど、ストレスに反応して緊張を誘発する物質や、過剰になるとうつ病の原因になるとされているマンガンが含まれています。⑪泣くとすっきりするのは、これらが涙とともに排出されるからだという説もあります。

111

Why can you drink many glasses of beer in a short time?

①Even if you can drink a few big glasses of beer without difficulty, it is not easy for you to drink the same amount of water in the same length of time. ②Why is it so?

③When you drink water, the water stays in the stomach for a while, flows slowly through the duodenum to the small intestine, and finally arrives at the large intestine where it is taken in. ④You can not drink a large amount of water in a short time: if the amount of water you drink exceed flow rate from the stomach to the duodenum, the water fills up the stomach.

⑤Beer contains ethyl alcohol. ⑥Alcohol is likely to be taken in through the mucous membranes. ⑦It is thought that the nature of alcohol helps 20 to 30 percent of the beer to taken into the stomach and the duodenum, where water is not taken in at all. ⑧Additionally, beer has two kinds of diuretic effects. ⑨The first is that alcohol cuts down on the

第4章　人間の体の疑問

production of a hormone which controls the amount of
　　　　　　　分泌　　　　　　　ホルモン　　　　　　　〜を制御する
ユウリン
urine. ⑩The second is the diuretic effect which the
尿
ポタシウム
potassium in beer has. ⑪You can drink a large amount of
カリウム
beer in a short time because beer is taken in easily and it

is excreted from the body quickly.
〜から排出される

問41　　どうして、ビールは何杯も飲めるの？

答 ①大ジョッキのビールを３杯くらい平気で飲める人でも、同じ時間で同じ量の水を飲むことは容易ではありません。②なぜでしょうか？

③水を飲むと胃に留まった後に、十二指腸を経て小腸、大腸とゆっくり送られ、大腸で吸収されます。④短時間に大量の水を飲めないわけは、水を飲むスピードに、水を十二指腸に送るスピードが追いつかず、胃をいっぱいにしてしまうからです。

⑤ビールにはエチルアルコールが含まれています。⑥アルコールは粘膜などから体内に吸収されやすい性質があります。⑦このアルコールの作用により、水が吸収されない胃や十二指腸で、ビールの20〜30パーセント程度が吸収されると考えられています。

⑧加えて、ビールには２つの利尿作用があります。⑨一つは、アルコールが尿を抑制するホルモンの分泌を抑える作用です。⑩もう一つは、ビールに含まれているカリウムの利尿作用です。⑪吸収のよさと、すみやかな排出により、ビールは短時間にたくさん飲むことができるのです。

Q42 Why does alcohol make people drunk?

①After you drink alcohol, your stomach and intestine take it in. ②Then alcohol gets into the blood and goes to the liver, where it is usually broken down. ③However, some alcohol which is not broken down and stays in the blood flows through blood vessels to the brain. ④This alcohol paralyzes the brain little by little. ⑤This state is drunkenness.

⑥As the blood-alcohol level goes up, the cerebral neocortex is paralyzed and then the paralysis spreads to the cerebral limbic system, the cerebellum, the hippocampus, and finally to the medulla oblongata. ⑦When only the cerebral neocortex is paralyzed, you are slightly drunk and flush a little. ⑧When the cerebellum is paralyzed, you become unsteady on your feet and can not walk straight. ⑨You sometimes feel like vomiting in this case. ⑩When the hippocampus, which is the center of the memory, is paralyzed, you can not speak well and you have a poor memory. ⑪Finally, when the medulla oblongata is

第4章　人間の体の疑問

paralyzed, you can not move your body and you are in serious
<small>非常に危険な状態で</small>
danger.

⑫In the course of time, alcohol in the blood is broken down in
<small>時間がたつにつれて</small>
the liver. ⑬The brain recovers from the paralysis and you come
<small>〜から回復する　　　　　　　　正気に戻る</small>
to yourself as this breaking down continues and the blood-
<small>進む</small>
alcohol level goes down. (see p.117)

問42　酒を飲むと、どうして酔っぱらうの？

答　①酒を飲むと、アルコール分はまず胃や腸で吸収されます。②続いて血液に入り肝臓へ送られ、分解されます。③肝臓で分解されなかったアルコールは、血液の中に残されたまま、血管を通り、脳に達します。④そして、脳を麻痺させていきます。⑤これが、酔っぱらった状態です。

⑥血液中のアルコール濃度が上がるにつれ、大脳新皮質→大脳辺縁系→小脳→海馬→延髄と麻痺が広がります。⑦大脳新皮質が麻痺している状態は、顔がほんのり赤くなるほろ酔い状態です。⑧小脳が麻痺すると足元がふらつき、まともに歩けなくなります。⑨吐き気を感じることもあります。⑩記憶中枢である海馬まで麻痺が進むと、ろれつがまわらなくなり、記憶が定かでなくなります。⑪そして、最後に延髄が麻痺すると、体を動かすことができなくなり、非常に危険な状態に陥ります。

⑫時間がたつにつれ、血液中のアルコールは肝臓で分解されていきます。⑬分解が進むと血液中のアルコール濃度が下がり、脳が麻痺から回復して酔いがさめます。

115

ヒトとサルは同じ祖先から枝分かれした

Human beings and chimpanzees separated from the common ancestor.

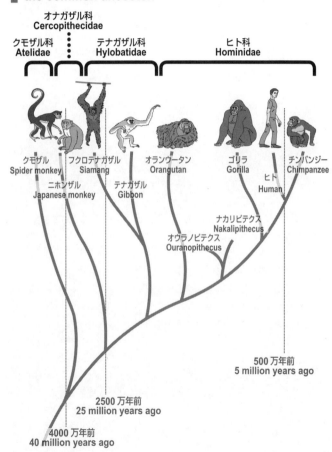

酒を飲むと、脳の麻痺が進むにつれて酔いが増す
When you drink alcohol, you feel drunk more as your brain becomes paralyzed.

ほろ酔い状態
Slight drunkenness

大脳皮質が麻痺
The cerebral cortex is paralyzed.

顔がほんのり赤くなる
You flush a little.

千鳥足状態
Tipsy stagger

小脳が麻痺する
The cerebellum is paralyzed.

足元がふらつき、まともに歩けない
You become unsteady on your feet and can not walk straight.

酩酊状態
Heavy drunkenness

海馬が麻痺する
The hippocampus is paralyzed.

ろれつがまわらず、記憶が定かでない
You can not speak well and you have a poor memory.

昏睡状態
Coma

延髄が麻痺する
The medulla oblongata is paralyzed.

体を動かすことができない
You can not move your body.

Q43   Why are feces brown?

①What you eat goes from the mouth to the small intestine by way of the gullet, the stomach, and the duodenum. ②Nutrients are taken in mainly at the small intestine, and the rest such as food fiber is sent to the large intestine with water. ③At the large intestine, water is taken in and the waste is excreted as feces.
④The coloring matter of feces is bilirubin, which is in bile made in the liver. ⑤Bile is made in the liver and goes through the cholecyst and the bile duct to the duodenum, where what you eat is mixed with bile.

⑥Bile acid is found in bile as well as bilirubin. ⑦Bile acid makes it easier to digest or take in fat. ⑧Bilirubin is made from broken-down hemoglobins of old blood, which is a kind of the waste. ⑨Bilirubin is also called bile pigment, and it is yellow. ⑩The color of feces comes from the brown color of stercobilinogen, which is made from bilirubin by intestinal bacteria, and the yellow color of

第4章　人間の体の疑問

bilirubin remained.
　　　　　残りの

問43　ウンチはどうして、茶色なの？

答　①食べたものは口から食道、胃、十二指腸を経て小腸に送られます。②小腸などで栄養分が吸収され、繊維分などのカスが水分と一緒に大腸に送られます。③そして、大腸で水分が吸収されたものが、ウンチとなり、肛門から排出されるのです。④ウンチの色のもととなる色素は、肝臓でつくられる胆汁に含まれているビリルビンです。⑤胆汁は肝臓でつくられ、胆嚢、胆管を経て十二指腸に送られ、そこで食べたものと混じります。⑥胆汁には、ビリルビンのほかに胆汁酸が含まれています。⑦胆汁酸には、脂肪を消化・吸収しやすくする働きがあります。⑧ビリルビンは、古くなった血液のヘモグロビンが分解されたもので、一種の排泄物です。⑨胆汁色素とも呼ばれるもので、黄色をしています。⑩このビリルビンから腸内の細菌によってつくられるステルコビリノーゲンの褐色と、残りのビリルビンの黄色がウンチの色となるのです。

119

Why do we dream?

①It is said that human beings dream mainly during REM sleep (rapid eye movement sleep), or light sleep. ②There are many hypotheses about why we dream, but the mechanism of dreams has not been clarified yet.

③The most popular hypothesis is that dreams have something to do with a brain wave called the PGO wave (Ponto-geniculo-occipital wave). ④It is known that the brain sends out PGO waves during REM sleep. ⑤There is a part of the brain which controls vision in the cerebral cortex. ⑥The hypothesis says that this part of the brain, stimulated by PGO waves, calls up visual images from memories in fragments.

⑦PGO waves are sent out not only from the brain of human beings but also from that of most other mammals during sleep. ⑧If this theory is true, cats and dogs are very likely to dream as well as human beings.

第4章 人間の体の疑問

問44　人はなぜ、夢を見るの？

答　①人間が夢を見るのは、主に眠りが浅いレム睡眠中だといわれています。②そのメカニズムについては、いくつかの説がありますが、はっきりとしたことはまだ解明されていません。③なかでも有力なのは、脳波の一種であるPGO波と関係しているという説です。④レム睡眠中には、PGO波が出ることが知られています。⑤大脳皮質には、視覚を司る部分があります。⑥レム睡眠中にPGO波がこの部分を刺激することにより、記憶の中から断片的に視覚的なイメージが呼び起こされたものだとする説です。

⑦PGO波は人間だけでなく、ほとんどの哺乳類が睡眠中に出すことが知られています。⑧この説が正しいとすると、人間だけではなく犬も猫も夢を見ている可能性が高くなります。

121

Q45 Why do we have fever, cough, and a sore throat when we catch cold?

①A cold is caused by disease agents such as germs and viruses. ②When these disease agents enter the human body, the body tries to protect its cells from the attack by them. ③This is what we call immune reaction.

④The first immune reaction is inflammation, which is the cause of coughs, sore throats, and so on. ⑤Today, it is made known that what causes inflammation is a protein generally called inflammatory cytokine. ⑥It is made by white blood cells named macrophages, which play a part in fighting against the disease agents. ⑦Cytokines attract white blood cells by inflammation and coagulate blood and stop the disease agents from spreading to other parts in order to keep the sickness from getting worse.

⑧Cytokine plays a role in fever, one of the inflammation reactions. ⑨When cytokines get to the brain, the

第4章　人間の体の疑問

temperature control center orders the body to raise its
体温調節中枢　　　　　　　　～に―するように指令する　　～を上げる

temperature. ⑩Rise in body temperature keeps disease
　　　　　　　　　　　～の上昇

agents from increasing and makes white blood cells work
　　　　　　　　増殖すること　　　　　　　　　　　　　活発に働くこと

actively, so the sickness is likely to be cured.
　　　　　　　　　　　　　　　～しやすい　治る

問45　風邪をひくと、なぜ熱やせきが出たり、のどが痛くなったりするの？

答　①風邪の原因となるのは、細菌やウィルスなどの病原体です。②病原体が体内に入ると、人間の体はこれらの攻撃から細胞を守ろうとします。③いわゆる免疫反応です。
④免疫反応として最初に起こるのが、せきやのどの痛みなどの原因となる炎症です。⑤炎症を引き起こすのは、炎症性サイトカインと総称されるタンパク質であることが明らかになっています。⑥これは、病原体と戦う役割を持ったマクロファージと呼ばれる白血球によってつくり出されるものです。⑦炎症により、白血球を呼び寄せたり、血液を凝固させて病原体がほかの場所に広がるのを抑えたりして、病気の悪化を防ぎます。
⑧発熱という炎症反応にもサイトカインがかかわっています。⑨サイトカインが脳に達すると、体温調節中枢が体温を上げる指令を出します。⑩体温が上がることにより、病原菌の増殖が抑えられるとともに、白血球が活発に働き、病気が治りやすくなるからです。

123

Q46 Why does a headache go away with medicine taken through the mouth?

①It is easy to understand that stomach medicine can cure stomachaches because it dissolves in the stomach. ②Then, how does medicine work when we take it for headaches?

③Medicine for headache such as aspirin dissolves in the stomach and enters the small intestine. ④After that, it gets into the blood and goes to all parts of the body by way of the liver. ⑤Medicine for headaches gets to the head, the painful part, through blood vessels 15 to 30 minutes after taking the medicine.

⑥One of the causative agents of headache and period pain is prostaglandin. ⑦It produces pain by stimulating the nerves. ⑧Over-the-counter medicine for headaches such as aspirin works to keep the prostaglandin from causing pain. ⑨This effect eases pain.

⑩To sum up, medicine for headaches taken through the

第4章　人間の体の疑問

mouth enters the small intestine and is carried to all parts
　　　　　　　　　　　　　　　　　　　　　　　 〜に運ばれる
of the body through blood vessels, and then it removes the
　　　　　　　　　　　　　　　　　　　　　　　　　 〜を取り除く
cause of pain and the headache goes away.
　　　　　　　　　　　　　　 頭痛が治る

問46　口から飲んだ薬で、なぜ頭痛が治るの？

答　①胃薬を飲むと、薬が胃で溶けるため胃痛が治るのはわかります。②では、頭が痛いとき飲んだ薬はどのように効くのでしょうか。

③アスピリンに代表される頭痛薬は、胃で溶け、小腸で吸収されます。④その後、血液に入り、肝臓を経て全身に運ばれます。⑤頭痛薬は、服用後15〜30分程度で血流に乗って患部である頭部に到達します。

⑥頭痛や生理痛の原因の一つとして、プロスタグランジンという物質があげられます。⑦これが神経を刺激することにより、痛みが起こります。⑧アスピリンなど市販の頭痛薬には、プロスタグランジンが痛みを引き起こすことを妨げる作用があります。⑨この作用が、痛みをやわらげます。

⑩つまり、口から服用した頭痛薬が小腸から吸収され、血液によって患部に運ばれ、これが痛みの原因を取り除くため、頭痛が治るのです。

Q47 Why doesn't the stomach wall dissolve in stomach acid?

①Strong acid liquid and an enzyme that breaks down protein named pepsin come out in the stomach. ②The strong acid liquid and pepsin digest substances so strongly that they can break down meat. ③However, they do not digest the stomach itself, a muscular organ. ④Why not?
⑤The stomach wall is covered with mucous membranes which produce mucus. ⑥Mucus is made up mainly of mucin, which is the cause of stickiness in fishskin, taro, fermented soybeans, and so on.
⑦A mucous gel layer a few millimeters thick is on the surface of mucous membranes. ⑧The gel is something like konnyaku jelly or gelatin. ⑨When mucous membranes are broken down by strong acid liquid or pepsin on the surface of a gel layer, new mucous membranes take the place of the old ones. ⑩The reason why the stomach wall does not

第4章　人間の体の疑問

dissolve in the strong acid liquid or the digestive enzyme is
〜に溶ける　　　　　　　　　　　　　消化酵素
that this gel layer protects the stomach.

問47　胃の壁はなぜ、胃酸で溶けないの？

答 ①胃の中には強い酸性の液とペプシンというタンパク質分解酵素があります。②これらには肉類も分解してしまうほど、強力な消化作用があります。③しかし、筋肉でできている胃自体は消化されることがありません。④これはなぜでしょうか？⑤胃の壁は粘膜で覆われ、粘液が出されています。⑥粘液の主成分はムチンと呼ばれるもので、魚の皮、サトイモ、納豆などのぬめりのもととなる物質です。

⑦粘膜の表面では、粘液が厚さ数ミリメートルのゲル層をつくっています。⑧ゲルというのは、コンニャクやゼラチンのような状態です。⑨ゲル層の表面で強い酸やペプシンにより粘液が分解されると、新しい粘液に置き換わるしくみが働いています。⑩胃の壁が強い酸や消化酵素の影響を受けないのは、このゲル層によって守られているからです。

Q48 Why does the head hurt after eating shaved ice?

①The headache you have after eating something cold is called an ice cream headache. ②There seem to be two ideas about why you get an ice cream headache.

③One of them is an idea which has something to do with nerve messages. ④When you eat something cold, information that it is cold in the mouth is sent to the brain through the trifacial nerve. ⑤The stimulus of ice cream and ice, which are very cold, are so strong that information about nerves is confused and sent to the brain as information that the head hurts.

⑥The other idea is that something cold causes inflammation of the blood vessels. ⑦A reaction to try to increase blood flow is caused to warm the inside of the mouth which is cooled down by the ice. ⑧As a result, this idea says the blood vessels in the brain become inflamed temporarily

第4章　人間の体の疑問

because the blood vessels in the brain suddenly swell.
　　　　　　　　　　　　　　　　　　　急に　　　太くなる

問48　かき氷を食べると、なぜ頭痛がするの？

答　①冷たいものを食べたあとに起こる頭痛は、「アイスクリーム頭痛」と呼ばれています。②なぜ、アイスクリーム頭痛が起こるのかについては、二つの説があるようです。

③一つは、神経による伝達に関係があるとする説です。④冷たいものを食べると、「口の中が冷たい」という情報が三叉神経を経て脳に伝わります。⑤アイスクリームや氷は非常に冷たいため、その強烈な刺激によって神経の情報が混乱し、「頭が痛い」という情報として伝わってしまう、というものです。

⑥もう一つは、冷たいものが血管の炎症を引き起こすとする説です。⑦冷たくなった口の中を温めるため、血流を増やそうとする反応が起こります。⑧そこで、頭の血管が急激に太くなるため、頭の血管が一時的に炎症を起こす、という説です。

夢は、レム睡眠時に見ることが多い

You dream mainly during REM sleep (rapid eye movement sleep).

レム睡眠の状態
During REM sleep

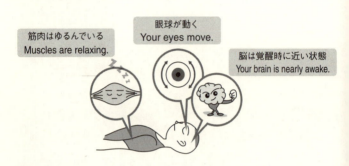

筋肉はゆるんでいる
Muscles are relaxing.

眼球が動く
Your eyes move.

脳は覚醒時に近い状態
Your brain is nearly awake.

夢を見るしくみ
How you dream

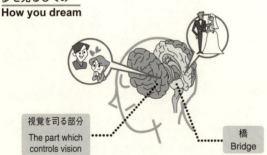

視覚を司る部分
The part which controls vision

橋
Bridge

脳幹にある「橋」から出るPGO波が大脳皮質を刺激し、夢の視覚イメージが生まれる
The PGO waves the "bridge" in the brain stem gives off stimulate the cerebral cortex and call up visual pictures of the dream.

かき氷を食べると頭痛がするしくみは?
This is how you have headache after eating shaved ice.

① 強い刺激で、脳が混乱する
The strong stimulus causes information in the brain confused.

冷たいという強い刺激が三叉神経に伝わると、脳が混乱し、「痛い」という情報になる

When information that it is cold is sent to the trifacial nerve, the brain is confused and thinks of it as information that it hurts.

三叉神経
The trifacial nerve

② 脳の血管が拡張する
The brain vessels swell.

血流を増やして冷えた口の中を温めるため、頭の血管が急に太くなり痛みを感じる

Blood flow is increased to warm the inside of the mouth and the brain vessels swell suddenly, so you feel pain.

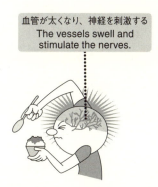

血管が太くなり、神経を刺激する
The vessels swell and stimulate the nerves.

131

Q49 Why do you have white hair?

①There is a hair papilla at the base of a
hair. ②Hair matrix cells, which grow hairs, are
around the hair papilla. ③Nutrients are sent to hair matrix
cells through capillary vessels and the hair matrix cells
divide to grow a hair.

④There are pigment cells called melanocyte around the
hair papilla. ⑤Melanin pigment which is produced in the
melanocyte goes into the hair, so clear hair becomes black.
⑥Hairs repeat the cycle of the anagen phase, catagen phase,
and telogen phase. ⑦The anagen phase lasts for three to six
years and hair grows during this phase. ⑧The catagen
phase lasts for a few weeks and hair stop growing during
this phase. ⑨The telogen phase lasts for three to four
months, during which the hair falls out and the hair matrix
cells get ready to grow new hair.
⑩In the telogen phase, you lose melanocyte with your hair.
⑪If you are young and have energy, melanocyte is

第4章　人間の体の疑問

produced to grow new hair and is placed around the hair
　　　　　　　　　　　　　　　　　　配置される
papilla. ⑫However, you have white hair when the

melanocyte is not properly placed and the hair is not filled
　　　　　　　　　　　　　　　　　　　　　　　～で満たされる
with it because of sickness, aging, stress, and so on.
　　　　　　　　　　　　　　加齢　　ストレス

問49　　　　　　**なぜ、白髪になるの？**

答 ①髪の毛のつけ根の部分には毛乳頭があります。②その
まわりに、毛髪をつくる毛母細胞があります。③毛細血管によ
り養分が運ばれ、毛母細胞が細胞分裂をして毛髪をつくります。
④毛乳頭の周辺には、メラノサイトという色素細胞があります。
⑤メラノサイトでつくられたメラニン色素が毛髪に入るため、
透明だった毛髪が黒くなります。
⑥髪の毛は成長期→退行期→休止期というサイクルを繰り返して
います。⑦成長期は3〜6年間で、この間に髪の毛が伸びます。
⑧退行期は2〜3週間で、髪の毛の成長が止まります。⑨休止期
は3〜4ヵ月で、脱毛の後、毛母細胞が次の発毛の準備をします。
⑩休止期に脱毛するときには、毛髪とともにメラノサイトが失
われます。⑪若くて元気なら、再び発毛するときにメラノサイ
トが作られ、毛乳頭の周辺に配置されます。⑫しかし、病気や
加齢、ストレスなどによりメラノサイトがうまく配置されなく
なると、髪の毛にメラニン色素がいき渡らなくなるので、白髪
になります。

133

Q50 Where do baby's feces go in the mother's body?

①A baby in its mother's body spends about 9 months floating in amniotic fluid in her womb. ②The baby gets nutrients and oxygen from the mother through the umbilical cord. ③The baby in its mother's body doesn't eat anything, so it has no feces. ④The baby drinks amniotic fluid through its mouth and urinates back into amniotic fluid. ⑤During this period, the baby keeps wastes, such as pieces of skin, hair, and so on, in its intestine. ⑥The first feces the baby excretes after birth are called meconium. ⑦Meconium is the waste of amniotic fluid kept for 9 months and it has a dark color and little smell.

⑧When the baby stays in its mother's body even after the expected date of its birth, the placenta doesn't work well and the baby has discomfort and feces float in amnionic fluid. ⑨If the feces go into the baby's lung through the throat, the baby sometimes has difficulty breathing and it

第4章　人間の体の疑問

gets into danger.
危険になる

⑩If it takes too long for the baby to excrete meconium after
　　～が―するのに―かかる

birth, the baby is likely to be jaundiced because the
　　　　　　～になりやすい　　ジョーンディスト
　　　　　　　　　　　　　　　　黄疸になる

bilirubin, yellow coloring matter in the meconium gets into
ビリルビン　黄色の色素　　　　　　　　　　　　　　　　　～に入る

the blood again from the intestine.

問50　お腹の中の赤ちゃんのウンチは、どうなっているの？

答　①赤ちゃんはお母さんのお腹の中で、子宮の中の羊水に浮かんで約9ヵ月間過ごします。②赤ちゃんはお母さんからへその緒を通じて栄養と酸素をもらいます。③食べ物を食べるわけではないのでウンチはしません。④口から羊水を飲んで、おしっこをまた羊水の中に戻します。⑤そのときに羊水に含まれる皮膚や毛などのゴミを、自分の腸の中にためておきます。⑥生まれてから初めて排泄するウンチを胎便といいます。⑦それは、9ヵ月の間にたまった羊水のゴミなどで、色が黒っぽくて臭いはあまりありません。

⑧出産予定日が過ぎてしまうと、胎盤の機能が低下し赤ちゃんが苦しくなって、羊水の中で胎便が出てしまうことがあります。⑨これが赤ちゃんの気管から肺に入ると、出産後に呼吸障害を起こすことがあり、危険です。

⑩また、生まれてから胎便が出るまでに時間がかかると、胎便に含まれる黄色の色素のビリルビンが腸管から血中へ再吸収されるので、黄疸になりやすくなります。

Why don't human beings breathe in water?

①Mammans such as human beings breathe with the lungs. ②There are many small bags named air sacs and they contain a lot of capillary vessels are in them. ③Air taken in through breathing goes through the throat and eventually reaches the air sacs. ④There, the air is taken in by blood flowing through the capillary vessels and, at the same time, carbon dioxide and water are exuded. ⑤This system does not work in water. ⑥Imagine that you take in water instead of air. ⑦When air sacs are filled with water, oxygen can not be exchanged for carbon dioxide in the blood. ⑧Furthermore, water goes into your blood when you take in pure water and water in blood comes out when you take in sea water, so the balance in the blood is lost in either case. ⑨This causes death.

⑩The baby in mother's body can live in amniotic fluid because it does not breathe with the lung but it gets oxygen

第4章　人間の体の疑問

from the mother and releases carbon dioxide to the mother

through the placenta.
　　　　　胎盤

問51　人はどうして、水の中で息ができないの？

答　①人間をはじめとする哺乳類は肺で呼吸します。②肺の中には肺胞という無数の小さな袋があり、毛細血管が集まっています。③呼吸することによって取り込まれた空気は、気管を通り最終的に肺胞に送られます。④そこで、毛細血管を流れる血液に酸素が取り込まれ、同時に二酸化炭素や水分が排出されます。

⑤このしくみは、水中では通用しません。⑥仮に空気の代わりに水を吸い込んだとしましょう。⑦肺胞が水で満たされると、血液の酸素と二酸化炭素の交換ができなくなります。⑧さらに、水の場合は浸透圧によって水が血液中に入り、海水の場合は逆に血液中の水分が流出して、血液のバランスが崩れてしまいます。⑨これは人間にとって死を意味します。

⑩胎児が羊水の中で生きていられるのは、肺で呼吸せず、胎盤を通して母親から酸素をもらい、二酸化炭素を戻しているからです。

137

Q52 How do you find a criminal by a fingerprint?

①There are no pores at the tip of a finger but there are sweat glands. ②The open mouths of the sweat glands are raised and they form a pattern of equal-spaced ridges like a contour map. ③This is the fingerprint.

④The pattern of a fingerprint never changes from the cradle to the grave. ⑤Even if you chip off the skin of the tip of your finger, the renewed tip has the same pattern of fingerprint as before. ⑥It is true that the finger grows thicker and the fingerprint grow bigger as people grow up but the pattern of the fingerprint never changes.

⑦There is no other person that has the same fingerprint as you in the world. ⑧You can not tell the difference between identical twins by DNA test but you can tell by their fingerprints. ⑨However, the fingerprints of identical twins are not completely different. ⑩They have similar patterns

第4章　人間の体の疑問

of fingerprint because they have same genes but there is
遺伝子
difference enough to tell one from the other.
一方と他方を区別する

問52　指紋でなぜ、犯人が見つかるの？

答　①指先には毛穴はありませんが、汗腺があります。②汗腺の開口部は隆起し、等高線のように一定間隔の隆線という模様をつくります。③これが指紋です。

④指紋は、一生変わりません。⑤たとえ指先の皮膚をはぎ取っても、皮膚ができると同じ指紋になります。⑥子どもから大人に成長すると指が太くなり、指紋も大きくなりますが、パターンは変化しません。

⑦また、世の中に同じ指紋の人は存在しません。⑧DNA鑑定で区別できない一卵性双生児も、指紋鑑定なら特定することができるのです。⑨ただし、一卵性双生児の指紋はまったく異なっているわけでもありません。⑩遺伝子が同一であるために指紋も似たパターンですが、指紋認証で区別できるほどの違いはあります。

Q53 Why don't we see things double though we have two eyes?

①We have two eyes, but we do not see things double. ②Why don't we see double?

③There is a crystal lens in our eye. ④Light passing through the crystal lens strikes the retina at the back of the eyeball. ⑤The image the retina receives is changed into signals by the nerves in the eyes lining up on the retina, and the signals travel to the cerebrum as two images on the right and the left.

⑥The two images which travel as the signals through the nerve to the cerebrum from the right eye and the left eye are overlapped by the following three functions of the cerebrum. ⑦The first one is simultaneous perception, which is a function allowing us to see two different images at the same time. ⑧The second is the fusion, which is a function which allows two images to overlap and make them into one. ⑨The third is binocular vision, which is a function which

140

第4章　人間の体の疑問

creates a feeling of distance and depth by small differences
　　　　　距離と立体の感覚
between the two images on the right and the left.

⑩Images produced on the retinas of the two eyeballs come
　　　　　　　　　　～の上に作られた　　　　　　　　　一緒になる
together because of these three functions of the cerebrum.

⑪That is why we can see things in 3D. (see p.144)
　そのため　　　　　　　　　　　　立体的に

問53　眼は二つあるのに、なぜものが一つに見えるの？

答 ①私たちには眼が二つありますが、見えている像は一つ
だけです。②これは、なぜでしょうか？
③眼には水晶体というレンズがあります。④水晶体を通過した
光は、眼の一番奥にある網膜に映し出されます。⑤映し出され
た像は、両眼の網膜に並ぶ視神経によって信号に変換され、左
右二つの像として大脳に伝えられます。
⑥大脳に備わっている次の三つの働きによって、右眼と左眼か
ら神経を通じて信号として送られてきた二つの像が重ね合わせ
られます。⑦まず、「同時視」は、二つの異なった像を同時に
見る働きです。⑧次に、「融像」は二つの像を重ね合わせ、一
つの像にする働きです。⑨そして、「立体視」は、左右の像の
微妙な違いから、像に遠近感や立体感を与えます。
⑩大脳が持つ、これら三つの働きにより、二つの眼に映し出さ
れた像は一つになります。⑪そして、私たちは立体的にものを
見ることができるのです。

Q54 Why can you see clearly with glasses?

①The human eye is like a convex lens. ②The focal distance changes according to the thickness of the lens. ③You usually move a magnifying glass back and forth when you look at something small through it to adjust the distance between the thing you want to see and your eyes equal to the focal distance.

④You can not bring your eye into focus by adjusting the distance between the crystal lens and the retina, which receives images made by the light passing through the crystal lens, because the distance between the lens and the retina can not be changed in the eye. ⑤Therefore you adjust the focal distance by changing the thickness of the crystal lens by the power of a muscle in the ciliary body.
⑥A near sighted person can not focus on a distant thing because he or she can not make the crystal lens thin. ⑦When the person sees through the glasses of a concave

142

第4章　人間の体の疑問

lens, he or she can see a distant thing clearly because this is
　　　　　　　　　　　　　　　　　はっきりと
in the same state as it is when he or she makes the crystal
　～であるのと同じ状態で
lens, the convex lens, thin.

⑧On the other hand, a far sighted person wears glasses
　　　　　　　　　　　　遠視の人
with a convex lens because the lens of his or her eye is the
　　　　　　　　　　　　　　　　　　　　　　　　　　　～と反対に
opposite of that of a near sighted person. (see p.145)

問54　メガネをかけると、なぜよく見えるようになるの？

答　①人間の眼は凸レンズのようなものです。②レンズは厚さによって焦点距離も変わります。③虫眼鏡で小さいものを見るときレンズの位置を調節するのは、見る対象と眼の位置をレンズの焦点距離に合わせるためです。

④人間の眼は、レンズである水晶体とレンズを通過した光が像を結ぶ網膜が一体化しているため、それらの距離を調整してピントを合わせることができません。⑤そこで、毛様体の中にある筋肉の力で水晶体の厚さを変えて、焦点距離を調整します。

⑥近視の人は、水晶体を薄くできないため、遠くに焦点を合わせられません。⑦凹レンズのメガネをかけると、水晶体の凸レンズを薄くしたのと同じ状態になり、遠くもはっきり見えるようになります。

⑧一方、遠視の人は近視の人と逆の状態なので、凸レンズのメガネをかけます。

143

眼は二つあるのに、なぜものは一つに見えるの?
Why don't we see things double though we have two eyes?

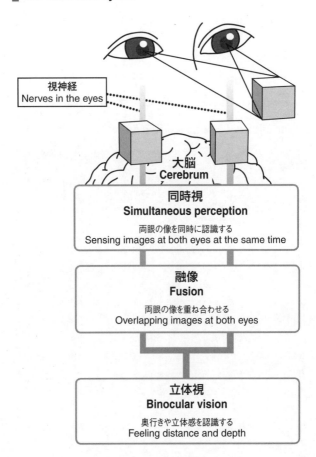

メガネは水晶体の焦点を補正する
Glasses correct the focus of the crystal lens.

正常な眼
Good eye

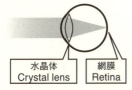

眼のレンズである水晶体の焦点が網膜上にあるので、光は網膜にはっきりと像を結ぶ

Light makes images on the retina clearly because crystal lens, the lens in the eye, has a focal point on the retina.

近視
Near sight

水晶体を薄くできないので、焦点が網膜よりも手前になる

They cannot make the crystal lens thin so the focal point is before the retina.

凹レンズで焦点を後ろにずらすと、はっきりと見えるようになる

They can make the focal point far with a concave lens and see clearly.

遠視
Far sight

水晶体を厚くできないので、焦点が網膜よりも奥になる

They cannot make the crystal lens thick so the focal point is after the retina.

凸レンズで焦点を手前にずらすと、はっきりと見えるようになる

They can make the focal point near with a convex lens and see clearly.

How do they check the blood types, A, B, O, and AB?

①Human blood is classified into four types, A, B, O, and AB. ②They are determined by the red blood cells and protein in blood serum. ③When you mix two different types of blood, you can find that some pairs clot and others do not clot.

④Red blood cells in blood have A antigens or B antigens in them. ⑤A person with A type blood has A antigen and a person with B type blood has a B antigen. ⑥A person with O type blood has neither of them and a person who has both of them is one with AB type blood.

⑦Blood serum, the liquid portion of blood, has two kinds of antibodies, α and β, which make red blood cells together in reaction to the A antigen or the B antigen. ⑧A person with A type blood has β and a person with B type blood has α. ⑨A person with O type blood has both of them. ⑩A person with AB type blood has neither of them.

146

第4章　人間の体の疑問

⑪When you mix two different types of blood, some pairs clot and others do not clot and you can determine the blood type.

問55　どうやって、A、B、O、AB の血液型を調べるの？

答　①人はA、B、O、ABの4つの血液型のどれかに分類されます。②それは赤血球と血清の中のタンパク質で決まっています。③血液を混ぜ合わせてみると、固まる組み合わせと固まらない組み合わせがあることがわかります。

④血液の中の赤血球には、A抗原またはB抗原が含まれています。⑤A型の人はA抗原、B型の人はB抗原を持っています。⑥O型の人はどちらの抗原も持っていない人で、両方の抗原を持っている人はAB型です。

⑦血液の液体成分である血清にはA、Bそれぞれの抗原に反応して赤血球を凝集させる物質である、二種類の抗体 α と β が含まれています。⑧A型の人は β を、B型の人は α を持っています。⑨O型の人は両方の抗体を持っています。⑩AB型の人はどちらの抗体も持っていません。

⑪混ぜ合わせたときの凝集の様子から血液型を特定するのです。

147

人の体はこんなに神秘的!
How mysterious human body is!

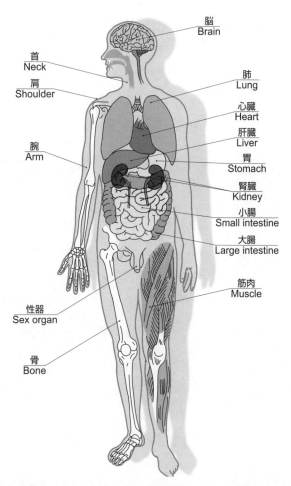

Chapter 5

Questions about the things around us

第5章

身の周りの疑問

Qustions and answers about science

Why can microwave ovens heat up food?

①There is an antenna-like thing, called a magnetron, in the microwave ovens which gives off microwaves.
②Any food has a lot of water molecules in it. ③A water molecule is made up of two positively charged hydrogen atoms and one negatively charged oxygen atom. ④When a microwave hits the water molecules, they vibrate and their temperature goes up because of friction. ⑤That is why food will be heated. ⑥Microwaves of this kind of the oven pass through dishes, which have no water in them, so dishes will not be heated. ⑦Therefore only food, which has water in it, will be heated and become hot.

⑧The number of times an electric wave vibrates is called frequency. ⑨The microwaves of this kind of oven have a frequency of 2,450 megahertz, and positive charges and negative charges alternate with each other 2.45 billon times

per second. ⑩This frequency is suitable for vibrating
1秒間に　　　　　　　　　　　　　　　　〜するのに適している
water molecules and heating food. (See p.162)
　　　　　　　　　　　温める

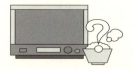

問56　電子レンジでどうして、料理が温まるの？

答　①電子レンジは内部に「マグネトロン」というアンテナのようなものが設置されていて、ここからマイクロ波という電波を出します。
②食べ物にはたくさんの水の分子が含まれています。③水の分子は、プラスの電気を帯びた水素原子が2個とマイナスの電気を帯びた酸素原子が1個からできています。④マイクロ波を水の分子に当てると、揺さぶられて摩擦熱が生じて温度が上がります。⑤その結果、食べ物が温められます。⑥電子レンジのマイクロ波は水分を含まない食器を、通り抜けるので温まりません。⑦そのため、水分を含む食べものだけ、発熱して温まります。
⑧電波が振動する回数を「周波数」といいます。⑨電子レンジのマイクロ波の周波数は2450メガヘルツで、1秒間に24億5000万回、プラスとマイナスが交互に入れ替わります。⑩この周波数が、水の分子を振動させ食品の内部まで温めるのに適しているのです。

151

Q57 Why do eggs get hard when they are boiled?

①Eggs get hard when they are boiled. ②The hardness changes according to temperature and time: soft-boiled eggs, hard-boiled eggs, and hot-spring boiled eggs. ③This is because eggs have protein in them. ④A medium-sized egg which weighs around 50 grams has about 6 grams of protein. ⑤Albumin, which makes up more than half of the protein in the white, and lipoprotein, which is in the yolk, are both proteins but their natures are different.

⑥The white starts to get hard at 60 degrees C and becomes soft-boiled at about 65 degrees C. ⑦Then, it becomes hard-boiled at nearly 80 degrees C. ⑧On the other hand, the yolk becomes hard-boiled when the temperature is kept at around 65 to 70 degrees C.

⑨Hot-spring boiled eggs are made by taking advantage of this difference between the natures of these two kinds of

第5章　身の周りの疑問

protein. ⑩When you keep the temperature of a <u>raw egg</u> at
生卵
about 70 degrees C for about 20 minutes, it becomes a hot-
spring boiled egg, whose white <u>is softer than</u> its yolk.
〜よりも柔らかい

問57　卵はどうして、ゆでると固くなるの？

答　①卵をゆでると、固くなります。②温度と時間を変えると「半熟卵」、「固ゆで卵」、「温泉卵」と、固さも変化します。③これは、卵がタンパク質を含んでいるからです。

④卵に含まれるタンパク質は、中ぐらいのもの1個（約50グラム）につき、約6グラム程度です。⑤そして、卵白に含まれているタンパク質の半分以上を占めるアルブミンと卵黄に含まれるリポタンパク質は、同じタンパク質でありながら異なる性質を持っています。

⑥卵白は約60度で固まり始め、およそ65度で半熟になります。⑦さらに、80度に近くになると固まります。⑧一方、黄身は約65度から70度くらいに保つと、完全に固まります。

⑨こうした2つのタンパク質の性質の違いを利用してつくるのが、温泉卵です。⑩生卵をおよそ70度の温度で20分程度保温することにより、卵黄よりも卵白が柔らかい、温泉卵になるのです。

Q58 Why does plastic cling film stick to something?

①Plastic cling film has no glue on it. ②However, it sticks close to a plate or something like that. ③Why can it do so?

④One of the reasons of this is that plastic cling film sticks close to something hard such as a plate because it is very thin and soft.
⑤When a molecule of something gets close to another molecule, they try to pull each other and stick to together. ⑥This is called intermolecular force. ⑦When you put a paper box on top of another paper box, this force acts between two molecules close to each other.
⑧Thin plastic cling film made from soft material sticks to the rim of a plate or a cup. ⑨It stick to the plate because of the intermolecular force.

154

第5章 身の周りの疑問

問58　ラップはなぜ、ぴったりくっつくの？

答　①ラップには糊はついていません。②にもかかわらず、お皿などにぴったりと密着させることができます。③これは、なぜでしょうか？

④その理由の一つとして、ラップが薄くて柔らかく、食器のような硬いものにぴったりと密着することがあげられます。

⑤ものの分子と分子が近づくと、お互いにくっつこうとする力が働きます。⑥「分子間力」と呼ばれるものです。⑦紙の箱を二つ重ねたときにも、接近した分子の間でこの力が働きますが、表面に凹凸があるため非常に弱いものです。

⑧柔らかい素材でできた薄いラップは、食器のふちに密着します。⑨その部分に分子間力が働くため、食器にぴったりとくっつくのです。

Q59 Why do tears come in your eyes when you slice an onion?

①If you put an unsliced whole onion close to your eyes, tears do not come in your eyes. ②However, when you slice an onion, it stings your eyes and you shed tears. ③Why does this happen?

④Onions have an element, isoalliin, in them. ⑤Isoalliin does not become volatile at room temperature and it does not sting your eyes. ⑥When you slice an onion, isoalliin changes into thiosulfinate because of an enzyme named alliinase. ⑦In an unsliced onion, isoalliin and alliinase are in different cells, so they do not bind with each other. ⑧When you slice an onion, these cells are broken and these two elements changes into thiosulfinate. ⑨Thiosulfinate is irritating and is likely to become volatile. ⑩This element comes into your eyes and you shed tears.

第5章 身の周りの疑問

問59 タマネギを刻むと、どうして涙が出るの？

答 ①切っていない、丸ごとのタマネギを眼に近づけても、涙が出るということはありません。②ところが、タマネギを刻むと眼にしみて、涙が出てきます。③これは、なぜでしょうか？
④タマネギにはイソアリインという成分が含まれています。⑤イソアリインは揮発性がなく、眼にしみることはありません。⑥タマネギを刻むとアリナーゼという酵素の働きで、イソアリインがチオスルフィネートに変化します。⑦刻まない状態のタマネギでは、イソアリインとアリナーゼは別の細胞にあり、混ざることはありません。⑧刻むことによって細胞が壊れ、この二つが混じってチオスルフィネートができるのです。
⑨チオスルフィネートは刺激性があり、揮発しやすい性質があります。⑩これが眼に入ることによって、涙が出るのです。

Why does food go bad?

①Food goes bad because the organic matters,
　　　　　腐る　　　　　　　　　　　　　有機物
especially protein, in it are broken down by
　　　　　　タンパク質　　　　分解される
bacteria called putrid bacteria and other microorganisms.
細菌　　　　　ビュートリッド 腐敗菌　　　　　　　　　　微生物
②There are a lot of bacteria in the air. ③There are also a lot
of bacteria on your hands. ④When these bacteria move to
food, they began to increase. ⑤Food for human beings is so
　　　　　　　　　　　　繁殖する　　　　　　　　　　　　　とても〜なので—
nutritious for bacteria that they can increase easily in it.
栄養価が高い
⑥When these bacteria break down protein in the food, it
gives off smelly gas such as ammonia and hydrogen sulfide.
〜を出す 悪臭のする　　　　　　アンモニア　　　　硫化水素 サルファイド
⑦Some kind of bacteria make toxins which cause food
　　　　　　　　　　　　　　　　　毒素　　　　〜を引き起こす
poisoning. ⑧This state is what you say meat or fish goes
食中毒　　　　　　状態　　　　あなたが〜というところのもの
bad.

⑨Rice and bread, which have almost no protein in them,
sometimes go bad too. ⑩This is caused mainly by bacteria
　　　　　　　　　　　　　　　　　　　　　　　主に〜によって
called grass bacilli. ⑪The grass bacilli are related to
　　　　　枯草菌　　　　　　　　　　　　　　　〜と関係がある
bacillus subtilis and they are everywhere. ⑫Even when rice
納豆菌　　　　　　　どこにでもいる　　　　　　〜するときでさえ
goes bad by these bacteria, the rice does not have a very

158

第5章　身の周りの疑問

bad smell and these bacteria do not make many toxins.
　　　　におい　　　　　　　　　あまり〜しない

問60　食べ物はなぜ、腐るの？

答 ①「食べ物が腐る」のは、食べ物の中の有機物、特にタンパク質が腐敗菌と呼ばれる細菌やその他の微生物によって分解されるからです。

②空気中には、細菌が漂っています。③また、人間の手にも多くの細菌がついています。④これらが食べ物につくと、繁殖を始めます。⑤人間の食べ物は、細菌にとっても栄養が豊かで繁殖しやすい場所だからです。⑥これらが食べ物の中のタンパク質を分解すると、アンモニアや硫化水素など、悪臭の原因になるガスを出します。⑦菌の種類によっては、食中毒の原因となる毒素を出すこともあります。⑧これが、肉や魚などが腐った状態です。

⑨タンパク質をほとんど含まないご飯やパンが腐ることもあります。⑩その原因となるのは、主に枯草菌という細菌です。⑪納豆菌の仲間である枯草菌は、ごくありふれた細菌です。⑫この菌でご飯が腐敗しても、極端な悪臭や毒素を出すことはあまりありません。

159

Q61   Why is a drainpipe s-shaped?

①The drainpipes under the washstand, the kitchen sink, and so on are S-shaped so that water is always standing at their curve. ②It is true that there are various shapes but all the drainpipes are designed to keep some water in the middle of them in this way. ③The water kept there is called seal water and it seals the drainpipe to keep away smells and bugs. ④This system is called a trap. ⑤Even if there is a trap in a drainpipe, it does not work when you let flow a large amount of water at one time and there is no seal water. ⑥This is a phenomenon called self-siphon.

⑦Siphon is a system that can fill a curved pipe with liquid and lead the liquid to the end point at a lower level than the starting point by way of a point at a higher level than the starting point. ⑧When you let flow a large amount of water at one time, the drainpipe and trap work as a siphon and the seal water kept there flows away. (see p.163)

第5章 身の周りの疑問

問61　排水管の形はなぜ、S字型なの？

答　①たとえば、洗面所や台所などの下の配水管はS字に曲がっていて、常に水がたまるようになっています。②形はさまざまですが、排水設備には必ずこのように、途中に水をためておく仕掛けがあります。③たまっている水は「封水」と呼ばれ、排水経路をふさいで臭いや虫などの進入を防ぎます。④この仕掛けは、トラップと呼ばれています。

⑤せっかくトラップがついていても、大量の水を一気に流すと水がなくなり、効かなくなることがあります。⑥これは「自己サイフォン」と呼ばれる現象です。

⑦サイフォンとは、曲がった管の中で液体が途切れないようにして、ある地点から高い地点を越え、出発点より低い終点まで液体を導くようなしくみです。⑧大量の水を流すと、配水管とトラップがサイフォンの状態になり、たまった封水が流れ出てしまうのです。

161

電子レンジはマイクロ波で、食べ物の水分子を振動させて温める

The microwave oven vibrates and heats water molecules in food with a microwave.

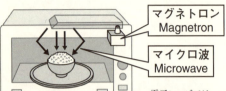

電子レンジでは、マグネトロンからマイクロ波を出している
Magnetron in the microwave oven gives off a microwave.

マイクロ波が食べ物の水分子を振動させる
Microwave vibrates water molecules in food.

水分子の振動で摩擦熱が生じ、食べ物が温まる
Heat is caused by the friction of water molecules and food is heated.

排水口に大量の水を流してはいけない理由

Why you mustn't let flow a large amount of water in the drainpipe at one time

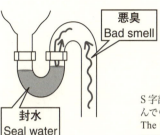

S字部分にたまった水が、下水から流れ込んでくる悪臭を遮断している
The water kept at S-shaped pipe keeps away bad smell from the sewer.

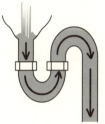

大量の水を一気に流すと……
When you let flow a large amount of water at one time …

▼

たまった水が、途切れることなく押し出される
The water kept there all flows away.

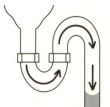

サイフォンの効果で、S字部分にたまっていた封水まで、流れ出てしまう
Water kept at S-shaped pipe also flows away by siphon effect.

163

Q62 What is the real color of shrimps?

①The striped pattern of shrimps in a fish shop is blackish. ②However, the striped pattern of boiled shrimps on the table is reddish. ③Why do they differ?

④Boiled shrimps looks red because they have a red coloring matter, carotin, in them. ⑤When you hear of carotin, you may think of carrots or tomatoes. ⑥The carotin of shrimps and crabs have is similar to that of carrots and tomatoes.

⑦The color of the striped pattern of uncooked shrimps is also that of carotin but it looks blackish, not reddish.

⑧That is because carotin binds with protein here. ⑨The carotin bound with protein looks dark red or green. ⑩When you boil shrimps, the binding between carotin and protein comes undone. ⑪As a result, carotin is back in its original color and shrimps come to look red.

164

第5章 身の周りの疑問

問62　エビの色は、本当は何色なの？

答　①魚屋の店頭に並んでいるエビの縞模様は、黒っぽい色をしています。②ところが、食卓に並ぶ、ゆでたエビの縞模様は赤っぽい色をしています。③これは一体、どういうことなのでしょうか？

④ゆでたエビやカニが赤く見えるのは、カロチンという赤い色素を含んでいるからです。⑤カロチンといえば、ニンジンやトマトが思い浮かびます。⑥エビやカニのカロチンは、ニンジンやトマトに含まれるカロチンに近いものです。

⑦生のエビの縞模様もカロチンですが、赤ではなく黒っぽく見えます。⑧なぜなら、カロチンがタンパク質と結合しているからです。⑨タンパク質と結合したカロチンは、暗い赤や緑色になります。

⑩エビをゆでると、熱によってカロチンとタンパク質の結合がはずれます。⑪その結果、カロチンは本来の色に変化し、エビが赤く見えるようになるのです。

What is the difference between fish with white meat and fish with red meat?

①Human muscle fibers are made up of red muscle and white muscle. ②Red muscle, which has a lot of red matter named myoglobin to store oxygen, has stamina. ③White muscle, which has instantaneous power and can contract quickly, has little staying power and gets tired soon. ④Human muscles are a mixture of red muscle and white muscle, so they look pink.

⑤The difference between fish with white meat and fish with red meat is a similar story. ⑥Tuna, mackerel, and sardine need to have stamina because they swim long distances. ⑦That is why they have a lot of myoglobin in their muscles.

⑧Flounder, sea bream, and so on, which don't swim long distances, need to get away quickly when they are attacked. ⑨That is why their muscles are white and have

第5章　身の周りの疑問

instantaneous power.

⑩Horse mackerel are sometimes classified with fish with
　　アジ　　　　　　　　　　　　　　　　　　　　　　〜に分類される
white meat because most of their muscles are white, but

they actually swim long distances and they are one of the
　　　　実際には
types fish with red meat.

問63　白身の魚と赤身の魚は、どう違うの？

答　①人間の筋肉繊維には、赤い色をした赤筋と白い色をした白筋があります。②赤筋はミオグロビンという、酸素を蓄える働きがある赤い物質をたくさん含んでいて、持久力があります。③白筋は瞬発力があって、すばやく収縮しますが、持久力に乏しく、すぐに疲れてしまいます。④人間の筋肉は、この白筋と赤筋が混じっているのでピンク色をしています。
　⑤白身の魚と赤身の魚の違いも、これと似ています。⑥マグロやサバ、イワシのように長距離を回遊する魚は、持久力を必要とします。⑦そのため、筋肉にミオグロビンが多く赤身です。⑧ヒラメや鯛のように回遊しない魚は、敵に襲われたときにとっさに逃げる必要があります。⑨そのため、筋肉は瞬発力がある白身です。
　⑩アジは、白身が多いため白身魚に分類されることがありますが、実際には回遊魚であり、赤身魚の仲間です。

167

Why do things burn when they are set on fire?

①Burning means that something binds with oxygen giving off light and heat in an intense manner. ②There are a lot of combustible things around us such as paper, wooden products and cloth. ③However, they do not burn by themselves if you do not set fire to them or heat them. ④Why don't they burn?

⑤Imagine that you move a lighter close to a dry wooden stick. ⑥At first, the surface of the wooden stick becomes dark brown or black, and then it gradually begins to burn with a flame.

⑦This wooden stick does not burn simply by moving a fire close to it because cool wood does not have any combustible element in it. ⑧If we heat it a lighter, the element of wood breaks down to become combustible gases such as carbon monoxide. ⑨Then, these gases start to burn with a flame.

第5章　身の周りの疑問

⑩Petroleum, gasoline, alcohol, and so on are easier to burn
　ペトロリアム
　石油　　　ガソリン　　アルコール　　　　　　　〜よりも燃えやすい
than wood or paper. ⑪These materials release easily
　　　　　　　　　　　　　　物質　　　　　　放出する
combustible gases even though they are not heated.
　　　　　　　　　〜だとしても

問64　　　**火をつけると、なぜ物が燃えるの？**

答　①燃焼とは、物質が激しく光や熱を出しながら酸素と結
びつくことです。②私たちの身の周りには紙、木製品、布など、
燃えるものがたくさんあります。③にもかかわらず、これらは
火をつけたり高温にしたりしないと燃えません。④これは、な
ぜでしょうか？

⑤ライターの火を乾いた木の棒に近づけるとします。⑥まず、
木の表面がこげたような色になり、しだいに炎を上げて燃え始
めます。

⑦火を近づけただけでは燃えない理由は、冷えた状態の木には、
燃える成分がないからです。⑧ライターの火で熱することによ
り、木の成分が分解され、一酸化炭素など、可燃性のガスにな
ります。⑨ガスが燃え出すと、炎が上がります。

⑩石油、ガソリン、アルコールなどは、木や紙よりも燃えやす
い性質があります。⑪これらは熱せられなくても、蒸発するだ
けで非常に燃えやすいガスになるからです。

169

Q65 Why don't pickled plums go bad though they are not dry?

①Food goes bad because of microorganisms such as bacteria. ②Almost all the microorganisms can not increase without water. ③Therefore people have made dry food by putting it outside of the house and removing water in the sun since early times in order to keep the food good. ④However, why do pickled plums go bad though they have water in them?

⑤Water in food has two kinds: bond water and free water. ⑥Bond water binds with the elements of food chemically, so it does not evaporate by ordinary way of drying and it does not freeze until around minus 30 degrees C either. ⑦On the other hand, free water binds with the elements of food weakly, so it can move freely and evaporate easily. ⑧Microorganisms increase with this free water and they make food go bad.

⑨One of the reasons why pickled plums are not likely to go

第5章　身の周りの疑問

bad is that they have little free water in them other than that
　　　　　　　　　　　　　　　　　　　　　　　　　　 〜のほかに
they are highly acidic and they have salt. ⑩Pickled plums
　　　　　　 強い酸性の　　　　　　　　　塩
sold in town sometimes go bad because they do not have so
町で売られている〜
much salt.

問65　梅干しは乾燥しているわけでもないのに、なぜ腐らないの？

答　①食品が腐るのは、細菌などの微生物によるものです。②ほとんどの微生物は、水分がないと増えることができません。③そこで、昔から食品を保存するために、天日に干して水分を除く乾物がつくられてきました。④ところが、梅干しには水分が含まれているにもかかわらず、なぜ腐らないのでしょうか。

⑤食品に含まれる水分には、結合水と自由水の2種類があります。⑥結合水は、食品の成分と化学的に結合しており、通常の乾燥法では蒸発せず、マイナス30度近くにならないと凍結もしません。⑦自由水は、食品との結合力が弱く、自由に動くことができる水分で、簡単に蒸発します。⑧微生物はこの自由水によって増殖し、食品を腐敗させます。

⑨梅干しが乾燥していないのに腐りにくい理由には、強い酸と塩分のほか、この自由水が少ないという理由もあります。⑩市販の梅干しが腐る場合がありますが、塩分濃度が低く抑えられているためです。

Q66 Why water changes to ice when it is cooled?

①Not only in water but also in any materials, molecules have a power to pull one another. ②On the other hand, they have a power to push each other and try to keep a certain distance when they move too close. ③This is a power called intermolecular force. ④Other than this, molecules have a nature to move actively when they got energy.

⑤The state of materials changes from gas to liquid, and then, from liquid to solid according to the balance between the molecular movement and the intermolecular force. ⑥Gas is a state in which molecules have a large amount of energy and each of them moves actively and freely. ⑦Liquid is a state in which molecules pull one another by the intermolecular force and don't move so actively because the molecular movement goes down. ⑧Solid is a state in which molecules stick close together and move little.

第5章　身の周りの疑問

⑨To cool water is to take heat energy away from
　～を冷やす　　　　　　～から—を奪う　熱エネルギー

water. ⑩The molecular movement of water which is taken

its energy away goes down. ⑪Therefore the distance

between molecules becomes small and the molecules stick

close together to become solid by the intermolecular
　　　　　　　　結果(〜になる)

force. ⑫This state is ice.

問66　　　**水を冷やすと、なぜ氷になるの？**

答　①水に限らず、物質を構成する分子にはお互いに引きつけ合う力が働きます。②近づきすぎると、今度は反発して遠ざけようとする力が働き、一定の間隔を維持しようとします。③「分子間力」と呼ばれる力です。④これとは別に、分子はエネルギーを得ると運動が激しくなる、という性質を持っています。

⑤分子の運動と分子間力のバランスによって、物質は気体から液体、液体から固体と形を変えていきます。⑥気体は、分子が大きなエネルギーを持ち、激しく運動してバラバラになっている状態です。⑦液体は分子運動が減少し、分子間力で互いに引き合い、激しく運動しない状態です。⑧そして、固体は分子間力で分子がしっかりくっつき、大きな運動をしない状態です。⑨「水を冷やす」とは、「水から熱エネルギーを奪う」ことです。⑩エネルギーを奪われた水の分子運動は減少します。⑪そのため、分子間の距離も小さくなり、分子間力によって、分子がしっかりとくっついて固体になります。⑫これが氷です。

173

Q67 Why does it get cold in the refrigerator?

①As noted before, the state of materials changes from solid to liquid, and then, from liquid to gas according to its energy and the intermolecular force. ②Pressure is also related to these changes. ③When you put pressure on gas, the intermolecular force is likely to work because molecules come close one another. ④As a result, gas changes to liquid giving off energy, or heat. ⑤When you ease pressure on it, the reverse takes place. ⑥That means molecules get cold and changes to gas taking in energy, or heat.

⑦These two theories are applied to the household refrigerator. ⑧A material called cooling medium is kept in the cooling unit of refrigerator. ⑨When pressure is put on the cooling medium by a pump that runs on a motor, the state of the cooling medium changes from gas to liquid giving off heat. ⑩The liquid cooling medium is shot up to

174

第5章　身の周りの疑問

the place of low pressure, so it changes to gas and
　　　　　　 低圧力
evaporates. ⑪It gets cold in the refrigerator because heat is
蒸発する
taken away in the process.
奪われる　　　 その過程で

問67　冷蔵庫はどうして、冷えるの？

答 ①物質は、それが持つエネルギーと分子間力によって固体、液体、気体と状態を変えることは、すでに説明したとおりです。

②この変化には圧力も関係します。③気体に大きな圧力がかかると、分子が接近して分子間力が働きやすくなります。④その結果、気体はエネルギー（熱）を出しながら液体になります。⑤液体の圧力を下げると、逆のことが起こります。⑥分子はエネルギー（熱）を使って冷たくなりながら気体になります。

⑦家庭用の電気冷蔵庫は、これら二つの原理を利用したものです。⑧冷蔵庫の冷却装置には、冷媒とよばれる物質が閉じ込められています。⑨モーターで動くポンプで冷媒に圧力をかけると、熱を出しながら気体から液体になります。⑩液体となった冷媒を、圧力が低いところに噴出すると、蒸発して気体となります。⑪このとき熱が奪われるため、冷蔵庫は冷えるのです。

175

水のエネルギーを奪うと、分子がしっかりくっついて氷になる

When energy is taken away from water, its molecules stick close together and it changes into ice.

水蒸気（気体）
water vapor(gas)

> 分子が大きなエネルギーを持ち、激しく運動してバラバラになっている状態
>
> The state in which molecules have a large amount of energy and each of them move actively and freely

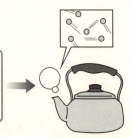

水（液体）
water(liquid)

> 分子運動が減少し、分子間力で互いに引き合い、激しく運動しない状態
>
> The state in which molecules pull one another by the intermolecular force and do not move so actively because the molecular movement goes down

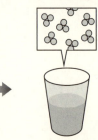

氷（固体）
ice(solid)

> 分子間力で分子がしっかりくっつき、大きな運動をしない状態
>
> The state in which molecules stick close together and move little

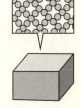

電気冷蔵庫は、冷媒が気体になるときの気化熱で庫内を冷やす

It gets cold in the refrigerator by the vaporization heat a liquid cooling medium gives off when it changes to gas.

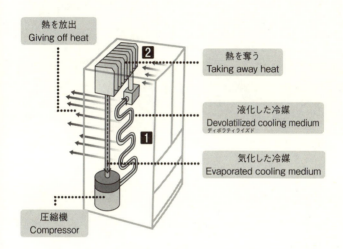

熱を放出
Giving off heat

熱を奪う
Taking away heat

液化した冷媒
Devolatilized cooling medium
ディボラティライズド

気化した冷媒
Evaporated cooling medium

圧縮機
Compressor

1

気体状態の冷媒は、圧縮機で圧力をかけられ、熱を出しながら液体になる。

Gaseous cooling medium put on pressure by a compressor changes to liquid giving off heat.

2

液体状態の冷媒は、圧力が低いところに噴出し、熱を奪いながら気体になる。

Liquid cooling medium shot up to the place of low pressure changes to gas taking in heat.

Q68 How can you see yourself in a mirror?

①There are some things other than a mirror which can reflect something. ②Some examples of these are windows glass, still water, and so on. ③Things which reflect something have a characteristic in common: their surfaces are even and smooth. ④Things which have this characteristic show specular reflection of light. ⑤Specular reflection is a reflection in which light from a certain direction is reflected at the equal angles. ⑥A well-polished brass plate also shows specular reflection of light but it does not reflect images as clearly as a mirror. ⑦A brass plate has a yellowish color because it takes in a bluish color, which is complementary yellow. ⑧You may say that polished silver and aluminum have a silver color, but in fact they are colorless. ⑨Colorless means that they reflect all colors in visible light in the same way. ⑩A mirror, which is made by putting a film of silver

第5章　身の周りの疑問

or aluminum on the back of a pane of glass, is colorless.
ガラスの板
⑪It has the characteristic of showing specular reflection of
light without losing any light and you can see yourself in
いかなる光も失うことなく　　　　　　　　　　鏡で自分自身を見る
the mirror.

問68　なぜ、鏡に姿が映るの？

答 ①鏡のほかにも、物体の像が映るものがあります。②たとえば、窓ガラス、静かな水面などです。

③像が映りやすいものに共通しているのは、表面が平らで、ツルツルしていることです。④こうした性質のものは光を「正反射」します。⑤正反射とは、入射角と反射角が等しくなる反射のことを指します。

⑥ピカピカに磨き上げた真鍮板も光を正反射しますが、鏡ほどきれいに像を映しません。⑦真鍮は、黄っぽい色をしていますが、これは黄色の補色である青っぽい色を吸収しているからです。

⑧磨いた銀やアルミは「銀色」といわれていますが、実はどちらも無色です。⑨無色というのは、可視光線に含まれているすべての色の光を、同じように反射するという意味です。⑩ガラスの裏側に銀やアルミの膜を貼った鏡は無色なのです。⑪それは光を効率よく正反射する性質があるため、きれいに姿を映すのです。

Q69 How does detergent remove dirt?

①It is difficult to remove greasy dirt on plates with only water. ②Oil and water naturally repel each other. ③However, when you use detergent, you can wash away greasy dirt easily. ④This is because the major element of detergent, surfactant, is working. ⑤The molecules of the surfactant are like very small matchsticks. ⑥The heads of these "small matchsticks" are likely to bind with water and the wood is likely to bind with oil. ⑦These "small matchsticks" come between oil and water so that they can bind with each other easily.

⑧When you use detergent, the part of the surfactant which can bind with oil first wraps greasy dirt in it. ⑨Many surfactants come close to greasy dirt and they break it down into small pieces. ⑩Next, water can come between the greasy dirt and the plate to remove the greasy dirt from the plate because the outside of the surfactant is likely to bind with water. ⑪The function that the surfactant

第5章　身の周りの疑問

mixes oil and water uniformly in this way is called
　　　　　　　　　　　　 均一に　　　　このように

イマルシフィケーション
emulsification.
乳化［作用］

問69　洗剤はどうやって、汚れを落とすの？

答 ①お皿についた油汚れは、水洗いだけではなかなか落ちません。②油と水はなじみにくい性質があるためです。③しかし、洗剤を使うと、油汚れが水できれいに落ちます。④これは、洗剤の主成分である界面活性剤という物質の働きによるためです。⑤界面活性剤の分子はとても小さいマッチ棒のような形をしています。⑥頭の部分は水になじみやすく、棒の部分は油になじみやすい性質があります。⑦これが水と油の境目に入って両方をなじませます。

⑧洗剤を使うと、まず、界面活性剤の油になじむ部分が油汚れを包み込みます。⑨たくさんの界面活性剤がくっついて油汚れを小さく分解します。⑩界面活性剤の外側は水になじみやすい部分なので、汚れとお皿の間に水が入り込んで汚れがお皿から離れていきます。⑪このように界面活性剤が、油と水が均一に混ざった状態にすることを乳化［作用］といいます。

Q70 Why can erasers erase letters?

①Pencil lead is made by mixing black powder, black lead, with clay and other things and by firing it at a high temperature. ②By rubbing it on paper, the powder of black lead sticks to the surface of the paper because of friction.

③Some erasers for pencils are made of rubber and others are made of plastic. ④When you rub this powder of black lead with a rubber eraser, the particles of the black lead on the paper stick to the surface of the eraser. ⑤When you keep on rubbing, these particles and the surface of the eraser become residues. ⑥Plastic erasers, which are softer than rubber ones, erase the powder of the black lead on the paper by encasing it.

⑦It is dificult to erase letters written with ballpoint pens with an eraser for pencils because the ink sinks into the paper. ⑧In this case, we use sand erasers, which are made of rubber containing fine sands. ⑨They can erase the letters

182

第5章　身の周りの疑問

written with ballpoint pens by chipping off the surface of
　　　　　　　　　　　　　　　～を削り取ること
the paper which the ink sinks into.

問70　どうして、消しゴムで字が消せるの？

答　①鉛筆の芯は黒鉛という黒い粉を粘土などと混ぜ、高温で焼いたものです。②紙にこすることにより、摩擦で黒鉛の粉が紙の表面に付着します。

③鉛筆用の消しゴムには、ゴム製のものとプラスチック製のものがあります。④ゴム製の消しゴムでこの黒鉛の粉をこすると、紙の表面の黒鉛の粒子がゴムの表面に付着します。⑤さらにこすると、これがゴムの表面とともに消しカスとなります。⑥ゴム製のものよりも柔らかいプラスチック製の消しゴムは、紙の表面の黒鉛の粉を包み込むようにして取り除きます。

⑦ボールペンで書いた文字は、インクが紙にしみ込んでしまっているので、鉛筆用の消しゴムではなかなか消えません。⑧そこで、ゴムに細かい砂を混ぜてつくった「砂消し」を使います。⑨インクがしみ込んでいる紙の表面を砂で削り取ることで、ボールペンの字を消すことができるのです。

Why can an iron smooth wrinkles?

①Cotton, linen and so on are held together by hydrogen bonds caused by the fact that oxygen and hydrogen, which form the molecules of fibers, pull each other. ②Hydrogen bonds are so weak that they come undone when they get wet during washing and their molecules are broken into pieces. ③When the cloth dries, it is rough and wrinkled because molecules bind with the nearest ones, which are different from before.

④Hot steam of irons is good for wool but it can not always smooth wrinkles in cotton and linen. ⑤A droplet of steam is one over fifteen thousand times as small as that of spray, so it passes easily through the gaps in fibers. ⑥Therefore the loose fibers of cotton and linen do not hardly get wet. ⑦By moistening these fabrics not with the steam of irons but with spray, you can easily smooth wrinkles in cotton and linen . ⑧Bound molecules come undone when you

第5章　身の周りの疑問

moisten the cloth. ⑨Ironing at that time makes water
　　　　　　　　　 アイロンをかけること
evaporate and the molecules bind with one another again
蒸発する　　　　　　　　　　　　　　　　　　　 互いに
without wrinkles because of the pressure.
　　　　　　　　　　　　　　　 圧力

問71　アイロンをかけると、なぜシワが伸びるの？

答 ①綿や麻などは、繊維の分子を構成する酸素と水素が引き合うことから生まれる水素結合で結びついています。②水素結合は弱いので、洗濯して水分を含むことにより解け、分子がばらばらになります。③水分が乾燥するときに、元の結合とは関係なく近くにある分子同士が結合するので、凸凹になり、シワができます。

④ウールには効果的なアイロンのスチーム機能ですが、綿や麻だとシワがよく伸びないことがあります。⑤スチームの水滴は、霧吹きの水滴の15000分の1というごく小さいもので、繊維の隙間をたやすく通過してしまいます。⑥綿や麻など目の粗い繊維だとほとんど水分が残らないのです。

⑦アイロンのスチーム機能を使わず、霧吹きで水分を与えてやれば、綿や麻でもシワをうまく伸ばすことができます。⑧水分を与えることにより、結合した分子がゆるみます。⑨そこにアイロンをかけることにより水分が気化し、圧力によりシワのない状態で分子が再結合するのです。

洗剤が汚れを落とすのは、水にも油にもなじむから
Detergent removes dirt because it can bind with both water and oil.

洗剤に含まれる界面活性剤の分子
The molecules of the surfactant in detergent

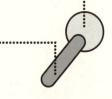

水になじみやすい部分
The part which is likely to bind with water

油になじみやすい部分
The part which is likely to bind with oil

汚れが落ちるしくみ
This is how dirt is removed.

1

界面活性剤が、油になじみやすい部分を汚れの表面にむけて集まる

The part of the surfactant which is likely to bind with oil faces to the surface of dirt.

2

界面活性剤が汚れを包み込む

The surfactant wraps greasy dirt in it.

3

少しずつ汚れを水中に取り出す

Taking dirt away into water little by little.

4

水ですすぐと、汚れは洗い流される

Dirt is removed by flushing with water.

霧を吹いた後、アイロンをかけると、繊維の分子がきれいに並ぶ

The molecules of fibers line up by ironing after moistening with spray.

凸凹になり、シワが寄った繊維
The fibers which are rough and wrinkled

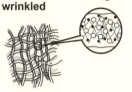

水素と酸素が不規則に結合している

Hydrogen and oxygen bind with each other disorderly.

シワが伸びるしくみ
This is how wrinkles are smoothed.

霧吹きで水分を与えると、不規則な分子の結合が解ける

When you moistening by spray, disorderly bound molecules come undone.

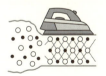

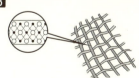

凸凹がなくなり、シワが伸びた繊維

Smooth fibers which are not rough or wrinkled any more

分子がきれいに並んでいる

The molecules line up.

Q72 Why does a magnet attract iron?

①A magnet attracts metals such as iron, nickel, cobalt, and so on. ②A magnet attracts them because these metals themselves became a magnet for a time by placing a magnet close to them.

③As you know from the fact that iron becomes an electromagnet when you wind nichrome wire around the iron, a magnet has something to do with rotation. ④In the molecules of metal, electrons rotate around an electron-shell at the center. ⑤A magnetic force is produced by these rotations of the electrons. ⑥However, in the case of most of the metals, electrons have their pair rotating in the opposite direction and the pairs cancel out the magnetic force of each other. ⑦In the case of iron and other metals, there are electrons which have no pairs, so a magnetic force is produced.

⑧However, iron is not usually a magnet. ⑨Imagine that there are countless tiny magnets in iron. ⑩The countless

第5章　身の周りの疑問

magnets are facing in different directions and cancel out
　　　　　 むいている　　 いろいろな方向を
the magnetic force of one another. ⑪By placing a magnet

close to them, they face in the same direction and the iron
　　　　　　　　　　 同じ方向をむく
becomes a magnet temporarily.
　　　　　　　　　　一時的に

問72　　　なぜ、鉄と磁石はくっつくの？

答　①磁石にくっつく金属は、鉄、ニッケル、コバルトなどです。②磁石を近づけることにより、これらの金属自体が一時的に磁石になるため、磁石にくっつくのです。

③鉄にニクロム線を巻き、電流を流すと電磁石になることからもわかるように、磁石は回転と関係があります。④金属の分子の中では、電子核を中心に電子が回っています。⑤この電子の回転によって、磁力が生まれます。⑥ただし、ほとんどの金属では、逆回りの電子が対になっていて、磁力を打ち消し合います。⑦鉄などでは、対になっていない電子があるため、磁力が生まれるのです。

⑧しかし、鉄は普通の状態では磁石ではありません。⑨鉄の中に小さな磁石が無数にあると考えてみましょう。⑩無数の磁石がばらばらの方向をむき、磁力を打ち消し合っています。⑪磁石を近づけることにより、その向きがそろって一時的に磁石になるのです。

Why does it become white when light's three primary colors are mixed?

①Visible light, which human beings are able to see, has many colors in it. ②They are the same colors as the many colors from red to purple in the rainbow, which is called the prism in nature.

③It is human beings that feel colors. ④The retina of the eye has three kinds of cone cells: L, M, and S. ⑤Red light excites L cones, green light excites M cones, and blue light excites S cones. ⑥Human beings can tell colors apart by these three kinds of cone cells. ⑦When these cone cells get a well-balanced stimulus, human beings feel it is white. ⑧In other words, the fact is not that it becomes white when light's three primary colors are mixed but that the color which is made from light's three primary colors is called white. ⑨However, the color white is neutral and is special for human beings. ⑩This is because white is the most

第5章　身の周りの疑問

commonly seen color and it is the color similar to direct
最も普通に見られる〜　　　　　　　　　　　　　　　　直射日光
sunlight.

問73　光の三原色を合わせると、なぜ白くなるの？

答　①人間の眼で見ることのできる可視光線には、いろいろ
な色の光が混ざっています。②自然のプリズムといわれる虹の
中に見える赤から紫までの色がこれにあたります。

③色を感じとるのは、人間です。④眼の網膜にはＬ、Ｍ、Ｓの
３種類の錐体細胞があります。⑤赤い光はＬ錐体を、緑の光
はＭ錐体を、青い光はＳ錐体を刺激します。⑥これら３種類の
錐体細胞によって、人間は色を見分けることができるのです。
⑦そして、これらがバランスよく刺激されると、人間は白であ
ると感じます。

⑧つまり、「光の三原色を合わせると白くなる」のではなく、「光
の三原色を合わせた色を白としている」のです。⑨にもかかわ
らず、私たちにとって白はニュートラルで特別な色です。⑩な
ぜなら、白は私たちが一番見慣れた、直射日光に近い色だから
です。

191

Q74 Why don't you get burned in a sauna bath?

①The temperature in a dry sauna bath is very high, around 80 to 100 degrees C. ②If you put your finger in boiling water at a temperature higher than 90 degrees C, you will get badly burned in no time. ③However, why don't you get burned in a hot sauna bath?

④The first reason is that it is dry in a sauna bath. ⑤When your body gets hot, you sweat. ⑥In a sauna bath, sweat exudes from your body because it is dry. ⑦When this happens, vaporization heat is needed and the heat of your body is used for it and your body will be covered with cool a layer of air.

⑧The second reason is that air doesn't transmit heat as well as water. ⑨When you put your finger in boiling water, its heat is transmitted to your finger directly and you will get burned. ⑩However, heat is not transmitted to your body directly when you take a hot sauna bath naked. ⑪The cool

第5章　身の周りの疑問

layer of air covering your body cuts off heat to some extent.
　　　　　　　　　　　　～を遮断する　　　　ある程度
⑫You feel pricking heat when you walk around in a sauna
　　　　　チクチクする～
bath because the layer of air partly breaks down. ⑬For
　　　　　　　　　　　　　　部分的に壊れる
these two reasons, you can take a sauna bath at higher than

90 degrees C for a long time without getting burned.

問74　　　なぜ、サウナでヤケドしないの？

答 ①乾式のサウナの中の気温は 80 ～ 100 度以上の高温です。②もしも 90 度以上の熱湯に指を入れたら、たちまち大やけどをしてしまいます。③それなのに、熱いサウナに入ってもヤケドしないのは、なぜでしょうか？
④第 1 の理由は、サウナ内部の湿度が低いことです。⑤体が熱くなると、人間は汗をかきます。⑥湿度が低いため、汗は体の表面で蒸発します。⑦このとき、気化熱として体の表面の熱を奪い、同時に体の表面に温度が低い空気の層ができます。
⑧第 2 の理由は、空気は水に比べて熱を伝えにくいことです。⑨お湯に指を入れると、お湯の熱が直接指に伝わり、ヤケドします。⑩ところが、高温のサウナに裸で入っても、熱は体に直接伝わりません。⑪体の周りにできた、温度が低い空気の層も、熱をある程度遮断してくれます。⑫サウナの中で動くと、チクチクするような熱さを感じるのは、空気の層が乱れるからです。⑬これら二つの理由により、人間は 90 度以上もあるサウナに長時間入っていても、ヤケドすることがないのです。

193

Why do clock hands move to the right?

①Clock hands move to the right because clocks were invented in the Northern hemisphere. ②There used to be various clocks such as water clocks, sand clocks, sun clocks, and so on before mechanical clocks, which have moving hands, began to be made.

③Among them, sun clocks were very popular. ④Sun clocks tell the hour by the shadow the sun makes. ⑤It is thought that the shadow moves to the right in the Northern hemisphere, so mechanical clocks were first made to move to the right.

⑥Not only mechanical clocks but also almost all meter hands move to the right. ⑦It is true that they were made to move to the right like a clock but moving to the right like the movement of the sun can be natural for the people living in the Northern hemisphere.

⑧There are quite a few left-handed clocks in the world such

第5章　身の周りの疑問

as the reverse clock in a barber shop, in which clients see
　　　　逆回転時計　　　　　　　理髪店　　　　　　　　　　　客
the clock in a mirror, and watches for special use.
　　　　鏡に映して　　　　　　　　特別な用途の
⑨However, people have difficulty accepting them partly
　　　　　　　　　　　　　　　　　　　　　　　　　　　　　　〜だという理由もあって
because they are used to clocks moving to the right
　　　　　　　　　　〜に慣れている
in daily life and think they are strange.
日常生活で

問75　　時計の針はどうして、右回りなの？

答　①時計が右回りなのは、時計は北半球で発明されたからです。②現在のように針が回転する機械時計がつくられるようになる前には、水時計、砂時計、日時計といった、さまざまな時計がありました。③なかでも広く使われていた日時計です。④日時計は太陽の影が時間を示します。⑤北半球では影は右回りに動くので、それに合わせて機械時計も右回りにしたのでしょう。

⑥時計に限らず、ほとんどすべての計器の針は右回りです。⑦時計に合わせて右回りにしたというだけでなく、北半球に暮らす私たちにとって、太陽の移動と同じ右回りのほうが、左回りよりも自然なのかもしれません。

⑧理髪店が鏡に映してみるためにつくられた逆回転時計や特殊な腕時計など、左回りの時計も存在しないことはありません。⑨しかし、常日頃から右回りに慣れており、違和感があるためか、ほとんど受け入れられないようです。

195

鉄の中の小さな磁石の向きがそろうと、鉄は磁石になる
When tiny magnets in iron face in the same direction, the iron becomes a magnet.

鉄
Iron

鉄の中には小さな磁石があり、通常はばらばらの方向をむいている。
There are tiny magnets in iron and they are usually facing in different directions.

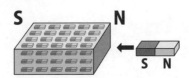

磁石を近づけると小さな磁石の向きがそろい、鉄が磁石になる。
When you move a magnet close to them, they face in the same direction and the iron becomes a magnet.

電磁石
Electromagnet

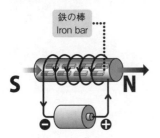

電磁石は、電気の流れにより、小さな磁石の向きがそろう。
In an electromagnet, tiny magnets face in the same direction by a flow of electricity.

サウナでヤケドしないのは、湿度が低いから
You do not get burned in a hot sauna bath because it is dry.

温度は90度以上あるが、湿度が低い
The temperature is over 90 degrees C but it is dry.

気化熱が奪われる
Vaporization heat is taken away.

温度の低い空気の層
A cool layer of air

サウナの中は湿度が低いため、汗が盛んに蒸発し、それが体の表面の熱を奪う。同時に冷たい空気が体表に層をつくり、その層が熱をある程度遮断してくれる。
Sweat exudes much from your body because it is dry in a sauna bath and the heat on the surface of your body is taken away. At the same time, a cool layer of air covering your body cuts off heat to some extent.

時計の針が右回りなのは、日時計が右回りだから
Clock was first made to move to the right because the shadow of the sun clock moves to the right.

北半球における日時計の影の動き
The movement of the shadow of the sun clock in the Northern hemisphere

北半球における太陽の動き
The movement of the sun in the Northern hemisphere

北半球では、太陽の移動が右回りに動くので、時計の針も右回りになった
The sun moves to the right in the Northern hemisphere, so clock was first made to move to the right.

Why does a playback of your recorded voice sound strange?

①When someone else is speaking, his or her real voice and a playback of the recorded voice sound similar. ②However, when you record your voice and play it back, the recorded voice sounds different. ③Why is this?

④A playback of the recorded voice travels through air to your ear, and then it is passed through the outer ear, the middle ear, and the inner ear finally reaching the auditory nervous center in the brain . ⑤This is called air-transmitted sound.

⑥When you hear your own voice, bone-transmitted sound, which travels through the vocal cords and the skull bone to the auditory nervous center, and air-transmitted sounds are mixed. ⑦So your real voice and a playback of your recorded voice sound different because of the difference in the way these sounds travel.

⑧The sound from a recorder travels as a air-transmitted

198

第5章　身の周りの疑問

sound. ⑨Therefore a playback of your recorded voice sounds more like your voice that others usually listen to.
　　　　　　　　　　　　　　　　　～のように　　他人がいつも聞いている～
⑩However, the recorded voice changes a little depending
　　　　　　　　　　　　　　　　　　　　　　　　　　～によって
on the kind of microphone and player. ⑪It is not easy to
　　～の種類　　　マイク
listen to your own voice as others listen to it.
　　　　　　　　　　　　　　　　～であるように

問76　どうして、録音した自分の声は変なの？

答　①他人がしゃべっている場合は、肉声と録音後に再生した声は同じように聞こえます。②自分の声を録音すると、生の声と違って聞こえます。③これは、なぜでしょうか？
④再生された声は、空気を伝わって耳に入り、外耳から中耳、内耳に伝わり、大脳の聴覚神経中枢へたどり着きます。⑤これは気導音と呼ばれています。
⑥自分の声は、声帯から頭蓋骨に伝わり聴覚神経中枢にたどり着く骨伝導音と、気導音がミックスされたものです。⑦このような音の伝わり方の違いから、自分の生の声と再生された声は、違うように聞こえるのです。
⑧レコーダーの音は、気導音として伝わります。⑨したがって、レコーダーで再生されたあなたの声のほうが、いつも他人が聞いているあなたの声に近いことになります。⑩しかし、マイクの種類や再生装置などによって、声が微妙に変わります。⑪他人が聞いているのと同じように自分自身の声を聞くのは、簡単ではないのです。

Q77 How are cell-phones connected?

①The cell-phone network is made up of cell-phones you have, base stations, the cell-phone switching station, and the lines between them. ②The base stations are equipment such as antennas which connect to cell-phones wirelessly and they are installed on the roofs of apartments or other buildings in your town. ③The base stations are connected to cell-phone switching stations by optical cable and similar devices.

④Imagine that you turn on your cell-phone. ⑤It connects to a base station and lets the cell-phone switching station know which base station's area it is in. ⑥The cell-phone switching stations record the position information which base station's area your cell-phone is in. ⑦When someone calls you, the cell-phone switching station finds the nearest base station using the position information of your cell-phone and calls your cell-phone by radio waves. ⑧Even if you move to another place within the area of

第5章　身の周りの疑問

the cell-phone network, you can talk on the cell-phone

because your cell-phone connects to the base station <u>by</u>

<u>itself</u> to update the position information in the cell-
自動的に　　～を更新するために
phone switching station. (see p.204)

問77　携帯電話はどうして、つながるの？

答 ①携帯電話は私たちの手元にある携帯電話機のほか、基地局、交換局、それらを結ぶ回線によって成り立っています。②基地局というのは電話機と無線でやりとりするためのアンテナを中心とする設備で、マンションやビルなどの屋上に設置されています。③それらは光ケーブルなどにより、交換局と結ばれています。

④あなたが、携帯電話のスイッチを入れたとしましょう。⑤電話機は基地局とやりとりして、どの基地局にいるのかを交換局に伝えます。⑥交換局はあなたの携帯電話がどの基地局のエリアにいるかを、位置情報として記録します。⑦あなたに電話がかかってきた場合、交換局は位置情報から最寄りの基地局を探し、電波であなたの携帯電話を呼び出します。⑧別の場所に移動しても、あなたの携帯電話が自動的に基地局とやりとりして交換局の位置情報を更新するので、携帯電話のエリア内であれば、どこに行っても通話することができるのです。

How can airplanes fly?

①When you hold a plastic board with sloping upwards to its front end and you run, you feel the power of the plastic board to try to move upwards. ②This mechanism is similar to that of flying airplanes.
③When an airplane moves forward, its wings catch the wind. ④The wind which passed by the wings turns down a little. ⑤As a result, it puts upward force on the wings. ⑥This is caused as a reaction force of downward flow of air. ⑦It becomes a lifting power to lift up the whole airplane.

⑧The wings of the jet airliners today is thicker than before and is curved artfully but the curved lines are different on the top from on the bottom. ⑨The lifting force is produced more efficiently by this artful shape of the wings. (see p.205)

第5章　身の周りの疑問

問78　飛行機はなぜ、飛ぶことができるの？

答　①下敷きのようなプラスチックの板を、前方が上になるように傾けて持ち、そのまま走ると、下敷きが上にあがろうとする力を感じるでしょう。②飛行機が飛ぶのも同じようなしくみです。

③飛行機が前に進むと、翼が風を受けます。④翼を通り過ぎた風は、少しだけ下方に向きを変えます。⑤その結果、翼には上向きの力が加わります。⑥下向きの空気の流れの反作用として生まれる力です。⑦これが、飛行機の機体を持ち上げる揚力となります。

⑧現在のジェット旅客機などの翼は厚みがあり、上面と下面が異なる複雑なカーブを描いています。⑨この複雑な形によって、より効率よく揚力が生まれるのです。

どこにいても携帯電話がつながるのは、交換局が すべての電話機の位置を把握しているから

You can talk on the cell-phone anywhere within the area of the cell-phone network because the cell-phone switching station knows where every cell-phone is.

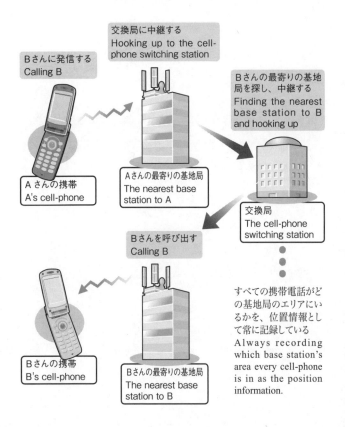

交換局に中継する
Hooking up to the cell-phone switching station

Bさんに発信する
Calling B

Bさんの最寄りの基地局を探し、中継する
Finding the nearest base station to B and hooking up

Aさんの携帯
A's cell-phone

Aさんの最寄りの基地局
The nearest base station to A

交換局
The cell-phone switching station

Bさんを呼び出す
Calling B

Bさんの携帯
B's cell-phone

Bさんの最寄りの基地局
The nearest base station to B

すべての携帯電話がどの基地局のエリアにいるかを、位置情報として常に記録している
Always recording which base station's area every cell-phone is in as the position information.

飛行機は空気の流れを揚力に変えて飛ぶ
Airplanes can fly by changing flow of air to lifting power.

プラスチックの下敷きを、進行方向が少し上になるように傾けて持ち、全速力で走ると下敷きが上にあがろうとする力を感じる

When you hold a plastic board with sloping upwards to its front end and you run as fast as possible, you feel the power of the plastic board to try to move upwards.

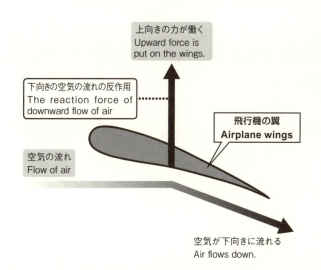

上向きの力が働く
Upward force is put on the wings.

下向きの空気の流れの反作用
The reaction force of downward flow of air

飛行機の翼
Airplane wings

空気の流れ
Flow of air

空気が下向きに流れる
Air flows down.

Is it possible to make a time machine?

①It is thought in theory that you can travel from the present into the future. ②Einstein's special theory of relativity is the basis for this and it says that time stops when it moves at the speed of light. ③This means that time would stop in a rocket traveling at close to the speed of light. ④Imagine that a 30-year-old astronaut travels to and from a star about 10 light years away in a rocket at close to the speed of light in 20 years. ⑤The astronaut comes back to the earth 20 years later and his classmates in school are 50 years old at this time but the astronaut is still 30 years old. ⑥This time delay at high speed was already proved by the fact that clocks run slow in a jet fighter. ⑦It may be possible to make a time machine to travel into the future by using this fact.

⑧There are various ideas about a time machine which would travel from the present into the past. ⑨However,

第5章　身の周りの疑問

today, most scientists think making it is impossible.
　　　　　　　　　　　　　それ(タイムマシン)を作ること　不可能な

問79　タイムマシンはつくれるの？

答　①現在から未来への移動は、理論的には可能だと考えられています。②その根拠となるアインシュタインの『特殊相対性理論』では、「光速になると時間は静止する」とされています。③光速に近い速度で飛んでいるロケットがあるとすると、その中の時間は止まっているという意味です。④仮に30歳の宇宙飛行士が10光年離れた星を、20年かけて光速に近い速度のロケットで往復するとします。⑤宇宙飛行士が地球に戻るのは20年後であり、同級生は50歳になっているのに、宇宙飛行士は30歳のままということになります。⑥こうした高速移動時の時間の遅れは、ジェット戦闘機の中の時計が遅れることなどで、すでに証明されています。⑦これを利用すれば、未来へ行くタイムマシンが実現する可能性があります。

⑧現在から過去へ行くタイムマシンについても、さまざまな仮説が立てられています。⑨しかし現在のところ、これは不可能だというのが多数の意見です。

監修者

松森靖夫（まつもり　やすお）

1956 年神奈川県生まれ。横浜国立大学大学院教育学研究科修士課程修了。現在、山梨大学大学院総合研究部教育人間科学域教授。専門は理科教育学。日本理科教育学会研究奨励賞受賞（1996 年）、日本理科教育学会賞受賞（2000 年）。
主な著書には、『論破できるか！子どもの珍説・奇説』（講談社ブルーバックス）、『科学　考えもしなかった 41 の素朴な疑問』（講談社ブルーバックス）、『学びなおしの天文学（基礎編・応用編）』（恒星社厚生閣）ほか、多数ある。

英文監訳者

Steve Mills（スティーブ　ミルズ）

1961 年ワシントン州シアトル生まれ。エンジニア。オリンピックカレッジ在学の後、米海軍原子力学校を卒業。専門の原子力分野だけではなく、自然科学から物理学まで、科学全般に造詣が深い。

カバーデザイン　杉本欣右／カバーフォーマットデザイン　志村謙（Banana Grove Studio）
編集　スタジオスパーク／協力　オフィスＯＮ／進行　磯部祥行

本書は、2010 年 7 月に小社より刊行された『素朴な「？」がよくわかる 英語対訳で読む科学の疑問』を大幅に改訂したうえ、文庫化したものです。

英語対訳で読む科学の疑問

2016 年 12 月 23 日　初版第 1 刷発行

監修者……………松森靖夫
発行者……………岩野裕一
発行所……………株式会社実業之日本社
　　　　　　　　〒 153-0044　東京都目黒区大橋 1-5-1 クロスエアタワー 8F
　　　　　　　　電話　【編集部】TEL.03-6809-0452
　　　　　　　　　　　【販売部】TEL.03-6809-0495
　　　　　　　　http://www.j-n.co.jp/
印刷所……………大日本印刷株式会社
製本所……………大日本印刷株式会社
©Studiospark, 2016 Printed in Japan
ISBN978-4-408-45682-9　（第一趣味）

落丁・乱丁の場合は小社でお取り替えいたします。
実業之日本社のプライバシーポリシー（個人情報の取り扱い）は、上記サイトをご覧ください。
本書の一部あるいは全部を無断で複写・複製（コピー、スキャン、デジタル化等）・転載することは、法律で認められた場合を除き、禁じられています。また、購入者以外の第三者による本書のいかなる電子複製も一切認められておりません。